America's Original Sin

America's Original Sin

Absolution & Penance

Arthur I. Montoya

Copyright © 2011 by Arthur I. Montoya.

Library of Congress Control Number:		2011912071
ISBN:	Hardcover	978-1-4628-4435-7
	Softcover	978-1-4628-4434-0
	Ebook	978-1-4628-4436-4

All rights reserved. No part of this book may be reproduced or transmitted in any form or by any means, electronic or mechanical, including photocopying, recording, or by any information storage and retrieval system, without permission in writing from the copyright owner.

This book was printed in the United States of America.

To order additional copies of this book, contact:
Xlibris Corporation
1-888-795-4274
www.Xlibris.com
Orders@Xlibris.com
100517

CONTENTS

Acknowledgements 9

Introduction 13

Chapter 1   I Am Not Black 19
Chapter 2   Founding Grandfathers 25
Chapter 3   Creating A White Nation 29
Chapter 4   Dredful Dred Scott 38
Chapter 5   Civil War Plus 44
Chapter 6   Forty Acres And A Mule 49
Chapter 7   Redemption And Cruikshank 53
Chapter 8   A Cotton Curtain 61
Chapter 9   Louisiana And "People Of Color" 66
Chapter 10   The Fourteenth Amendment 70
Chapter 11   Railroads And Mr. Plessy 73
Chapter 12   The Spanish American War 78
Chapter 13   Playing The Race Card 84
Chapter 14   Heroes And Warriors 94
Chapter 15   Roadblocks To Glory 101
Chapter 16   Integration Of The Armed Forces 105
Chapter 17   The American G.I. Bill Of Rights 114
Chapter 18   Vietnam 118
Chapter 19   Robeson To Robinson 121

Chapter 20	Black Hard Times	125
Chapter 21	Segregation Now, Segregation Forever	130
Chapter 22	Integration Now, Integration Forever	134
Chapter 23	The Murder Of Emmett Till	137
Chapter 24	The Greatest Generation And Fair Housing	144
Chapter 25	Kerner Report	149
Chapter 26	The Solution	164

| Appendix | The Constitution Of The United States | 169 |
| Bibliography | | 173 |

Dedication

This book is dedicated to:

Clay Tribble, my boyhood friend from Coachella Valley Union
High School
May he Rest in Peace

Harold L. Wilson
My loyal friend who has always been "tried and true"

ACKNOWLEDGEMENTS

I want to thank my nephew Kevin Beal, UC Berkeley graduate and history teacher who guided me in the early days of my transcript and a special thanks to my daughter, Irene Montoya Taylor and her wonderful husband, Nathan, UC Davis graduates and great English teachers who made my book read like a book.

First Reading: John 20:23

Whose sins you forgive are forgiven them, and whose sins you retain are retained.

Second Reading: 2 Chronicles 7:14

. . . and if my people, upon whom my name has been pronounced, humble themselves and pray, and seek my presence and turn from their evil ways, I will hear them from heaven and pardon their sins and revive their land.

Introduction

I never really knew Clay Tribble. Clay and I began kindergarten together at the El Campo farm labor camp grade school in Indio, California during the later years of World War II. I remember him vividly with his short hair and the little peak in front, but I remember him most as the toughest kid in class. Not the biggest or strongest, just the toughest. Clay took a liking to me and my brothers and we remained friends his entire life.

We went to the same grade school together through the fifth grade where Clay had an almost obsessive need to take care of me perhaps because I was the youngest in our class. My mother enrolled me in school a year early, so she could work to support the war effort; therefore, I was a young four year old amongst the five year olds. I have a vivid memory of kids teasing me after wetting my pants in the first grade. Actually, I did more than just wet, but I am too ashamed to admit it. Then, there was my faithful friend and hero Clay who stood between me and the other boys who were laughing at me. They might pick on a younger kid, but no one would challenge Clay Tribble. He kindly took me to the boys' restroom where I could clean up. Clay would remind me of this in the years to come, but he never mentioned it in front of anyone else. It was something that bonded us.

Clay, being my friend, was my security blanket. My folks and my brothers liked Clay. After we left the farm labor camp, my family and I lived on a farm about 10 miles outside town and were bused to school. Sometime in the fourth or fifth grade, Clay decided that he would accompany me home. He simply got on the bus one afternoon and went home with me. That evening he joined my family for dinner, slept over, ate breakfast with us the next morning and boarded the bus to school.

We had no phones in those days, and I am sure that Clay's family had no phone. We had no way to contact them that Clay was alright and would be staying with us. I never found out if he got in trouble or if his folks ever found out, or cared, where he was all night.

I never met Clay's folks nor did I know if he had brothers or sisters. I had no idea exactly where he lived as I never set foot in his house. He never invited me nor did he ever invite me to his neighborhood.

We played high school football together where he earned the reputation as the best pound per pound football player to ever play for our high school. The designee of "best pound per pound" player is always given to a smaller person, as a 250 pound person is never known as the "best pound per pound" player. Clay was about 5 foot, 8 inches and weighed about 155 pounds soaking wet.

We graduated in 1956 and I, along with three other classmates, decided to go to a community college in Orange County. I don't recall how it came about, but Clay decided to join us. He and I reported a month early to try out for the college football team where the head coach, Al Irwin, was a long time resident of the area. His grandparents had property right on the beach, a two story building where beachfront businesses were on the street floor and apartments were upstairs.

He understood that we needed housing and offered to rent us an upstairs apartment, designed to house five students. The coach told us, however, that Clay could not stay with us as the area was restricted and no blacks could rent there. He offered Clay a room in one of two dormitories on campus and Clay accepted. I remember that moment quite clearly and it is to my shame that I accepted the reality of the times. Clay did, as he did not oppose the action. I suppose I rationalized that if Clay didn't mind, who was I to make a big deal of it? It was my first experience of the two Americas, one white and one black.

This was 1956, in California, and two years after Brown vs. Board of Education. Two years after the hero of our times Earl Warren, Chief Justice of the U.S. Supreme Court and former Governor of California declared "separate but equal" unconstitutional. This was 1956 and a black person could not rent an apartment in Newport Beach, California.

At least two or three days each week, Clay would go home with me after football practice and have dinner with me and our other high school friends. He never once complained, never exhibited anger or disappointment as to his lot. Clay made first string on our championship football team, although he was a small guy. Small but fierce! I played just enough to earn a letter.

Clay majored in Industrial Arts; however, as anyone who goes to college understands, there are some core subjects that everyone has to take (i.e. English, History, Math and a general science course.) Clay struggled with those subjects and asked me for help with his homework. I was astounded to learn that Clay's reading comprehension was at the fourth grade level. He could not read a newspaper, a sports magazine or a textbook. As he so courteously did for me, I never mentioned this to anyone and felt honored he shared his shortcomings with me.

In high school, Clay played football and was all-conference. He lettered in baseball and basketball and was voted the Most Outstanding Athlete in our class and he could not read or write beyond the fourth grade level.

My dream was to become a school teacher as they were my best role models. I have no idea what Clay's dreams were. Clay played football for Orange Coast College, helped us win a championship and go to a bowl game. He quit college after that fall semester, went home and became a skilled cement finisher. He married, had a family and died before he was 50 years old.

Clay Tribble was my best and oldest friend and I hardly knew him. He was black, and I was not.

1948. The author, Art Montoya, in the 4th grade, Indio, California is the third boy, bottom row, from the left. Clay Tribble, is the black boy, 2nd from the left, back row.

1956: Hamilton High School, Memphis, Tennessee. The Choral Group of Hamilton High School with Harold L. Wilson, 2nd row, 2nd from the left just behind the girl in the white blouse. Harold was in the Honor Society, football, basketball and baseball teams.

1956: National Honor Society, Hamilton High School, Memphis, Tennessee. Harold Wilson is the young man on the far right. Harold went on to Tuskegee Institute, Memphis State University and earned a Masters Degree at California State University, Dominguez Hills, California.

The author, Arthur I. Montoya and his friend, Harold L. Wilson.

1

I Am Not Black

My grandparents were all born in Mexico. I am a second generation American as both my parents were born in the United States. I never knew my paternal grandparents, but was profoundly influenced by my grandfather Natividad through his son, Benjamin, my father. Natividad was a literate man and proud of his adopted country—America. He worked as a farmer, helped build state highways, and headed the maintenance department at New Mexico A&M College. He also served on the county school board, and always emphasized education's value amongst his children, which is a legacy my father passed on to me. I am my father's son.

Values and "rules of life" came from Dad, values and rules he learned from his father.

> Rule No. 1: Wake up early and rise before the sun.

> Rule No. 2: Work hard, because it is good for you.

> Rule No. 3: Take responsibility for your work and seek more responsibility.

Honesty was a given. From the paternal side, I received my individuality; from the maternal side, I received love, family and the pleasure of belonging to a great group. My childhood memories are filled with my mother and father working alongside each other in the fields and packing houses of the Coachella Valley. Our conversations were filled with sports, trivia, and laughter. We playfully argued over each other's favorite sports teams. Of course, no day would be complete without the family, extended and immediate, gathering around my mother's dinner table to share in the fruits of our labor. Our family worked together, prayed and played together and enjoyed each other's accomplishments. We lived for the enjoyment of each other.

My parents were participants, not spectators, of my early school years. The grades I earned mattered and the little line on the report card designating "Deportment" or "Gets along well with others" was equally as important as a grade in spelling, arithmetic or social studies. Recently, a friend sent me a picture that brought back memories of the 1955 high school baseball season showing my teammates waiting for their turn at bat. In the bleachers, one can clearly see my mother and grandfather watching the game. My father is a few feet away, among other gentlemen, watching the game and talking under a small cluster of shady trees.

My parents' involvement in our schooling was extensive. My mother knew the name of every teacher and coach we had. They required that I behaved, earned good grades, played sports by the rules, but played well enough to not sit on the bench. Second stringers were an especially bad thing to be in my Dad's eyes.

My parents taught us to never quit and always do our best, which was a life lesson that my coaches and teachers enriched in us. From my high school baseball coach, Charles Pryor, I learned that winning is a lot more fun than losing—but it was from losing that the best lessons were learned. Never blame the umpire, or luck, or the weather. He continually reminded the team that we won or lost on the basis of our play. We either played well enough to win or we didn't. Coach Pryor taught me to "want the ball hit my way" and to trust myself to make the play. I should always anticipate my response before the ball was hit. I later realized that he was truly teaching us that preparation, anticipation and execution were the keys of success in life, as well as baseball. As I moved forward in life and business, I applied these lessons for job interviews and career decisions. I was always prepared and ready to anticipate the company needs.

In college, my lessons continued. I was an offensive lineman and learned from my line coach the rules of Split T football line play that I remember more than 50 years later—"never let a man play you on the outside or let him beat you to the inside." My football coach, Steve Musseau, drilled us on the adage that "the battle doesn't always go to the swiftest or the strongest, but to the one who thinks he can!"

What is the point of all this? I learned early in life that there were keys to success and that principles did exist that gave the best chance to succeed. The following American values were instilled in me throughout my life—"the harder you work, the luckier you get," "study hard and get good grades, and you will succeed in life," and "hard work and good attendance will guarantee one a stable, good job." My dad also had a saying that "if you work for someone, work hard, give them more than they ask because the employer deserved it."

For the most part, these were the keys to my success and lessons I passed on to my children. Any success that I have enjoyed is in part my own doing, but for the most part, a result of great parenting, coaching by teachers along the way and lessons learned from folks who cared. Any shortcomings were of my own doing. I had the best opportunities to succeed because I am not black.

When I found time between baseball and football, I attended classes and shall always remember a lesson taught by my high school Spanish teacher, Miss McCallum. She was a veteran teacher who had never married. Short with a tight severe bun, she gave me the grade I earned in her Spanish I class—an F. I ended up repeating the class with another teacher and passed. In my senior year, I went back to Ms. McCallum for Spanish II to finish my graduation requirements. This time our relationship was different. She encouraged me to attend college and shared her own stories of world travels. In discussing world events in the 1950's, she commented that "there are but three major political issues in America—War and Peace, Bread and Butter, and Black and White." I don't know why I remembered this, but it obviously left me with a great impression.

In the 50 plus years since, I have witnessed that she was right, but am dumbfounded that we have never solved the issue of "black and white." Certainly the issues of war and peace and bread and butter are not totally in the control of our country alone, as we are part of the world, but the issue of black and white is ours and ours alone.

We invented, or inherited, the problem and not being able to solve it is unacceptable in this most Christian of nations, in the most caring, benevolent, exceptional and enlightened country on earth.

How big a problem do we have? The information provided is from Bureau of Justice Statistics, SPECIAL REPORT, dated August 2003 and other information as noted.

- There are approximately 2 million people in American prisons and jails, nearly 1 million are black.*

- The rate of imprisonment for black people is 845 people per 100,000 black population; the rate for white people is 145 per 100,000 white population.*

- At year end 2005, over 4.9 million people were under Federal, State or local probation or parole jurisdiction. 30 percent of the folks on probation were black and 40 percent of folks on parole were black. Blacks are 12 percent of the U.S. population.*

- In 1994, there were 7.66 Black Americans in federal or state prisons for every white, up from a ratio of 6.88 to 1 in 1988.*

- On a given day, 1 of every 3 Black American men in their 20s is under the control of the criminal justice system—in prison, on probation or on parole.*

- Black Americans compose 13 percent of monthly drug **users** in the United States; however, they account for 35 percent of arrests for drug possession, 55 percent of drug-related convictions, and 74 percent of the drug-related prison sentences handed out.*

- Between 1986 and 1991, the number of black women in state prisons for drug offenses rose by 828 percent.*

- Blacks are three times more likely than Hispanics and five times more likely than whites to be in jail.*

- There are more blacks living in prisons than living in college dorms.*[1]

- Black Americans represent 3.6 percent of all lawyers and judges in the United States.[2]

- There are over 3 million teachers in the United States, teaching K-12 students; only 7.0 percent are African-Americans.[3]

- Blacks attend the poorest schools, with the least experienced teachers, earn the lowest test scores and have the highest dropout rates.

- On average, African American and Hispanic twelfth-grade students read at approximately the same level as white eighth graders.[4]

- Drop out rates for black high school students is 50%.[5]

- The median income level for blacks is the lowest in the nation.

---

[1] Data asterisked * are from the Bureau of Justice Statistics, SPECIAL REPORT, August 2003

[2] Sherrilyn A. Ifill. "Judging the Judges: Racial Diversity, Impartiality and Representation on State Trial Courts. BCL.Rev.95 (1998). http//landigitalcommons.bc.edu/bclr/vol39/iss1/3 retrieved o8/02/2011

[3] http://nces.ed.gov/survey/sass. Internet release date 12/15/2010

[4] U.S. Department of Education, Office of Vocational and Adult Education, 2002) Alliance for Excellent Education FACT SHEET, April 2007. www.all4ed.org retrieved August 1, 2011

[5] Ibid

- The life span of blacks is seven years less than whites.

- . . ."the median wealth of white households is now 20 times that of black households, making the gap nearly twice the size it was in the two decades before the Great Recession."[6]

There are other quantifiable data and trends that would indicate that black Americans are at the bottom of the socio-economic ladder of U.S. society and will continue to stay there unless an outside influence addresses and removes the root causes.

Blacks certainly have excelled in athletics, but why haven't they excelled in greater numbers in business, academia, literature, and other economic areas in American society? How many black school teachers do you know? Where are the black scientists, engineers, physicians, and nurses, pharmacists, architects, builders, lawyers and judges, stockbrokers and bankers?

The root source of the problem lies in our American history and the black/white experience in that history. This country was founded on two fundamental Christian principles—we are all God's children and that freedom is a gift from God. But even in our country's infancy, America specifically excluded Negros. These beliefs mark the birth of our country and the birth of America's original sin. I believe I have *the only* solution that will forevermore settle the "black and white" problem that has burdened this country since the first black slave was brought on shore in 1619.

Why is it imperative that we solve this problem? First is that there is untapped potential in our midst that is needed to keep our country competitive in the new "global economy." Thomas Friedman, author of *The World is Flat*, describes the global advances in education and technology that threaten American economy, yet he offers the hope of innovation as a wellspring for American competitiveness.

Second is that the incarceration of people is a waste of human resources that suck up the economic resources of our country. Finally, the hope that will be instilled to millions of our brethren will breathe new life to the American dream. I am convinced by empirical evidence that there are no more loyal Americans than our black brethren and regardless of their experiences, they continue to love this country and have countless times given the full measure of devotion for our country.

The election of Barack Obama as the 44th President of the United States has only proven that anything is possible in our great country, but it does not in any way solve

---

[6] Rana Forohar. 'The Curious Capitalist," TIME MAGAZINE, August 15, 2011. Page 26

the "black and white" issue of our beloved United States of America. America's original sin continues to haunt us and will forever until we acknowledge the problem and repent. Absolution and resolution will come, but only after we pay the penance required.

This resolution to our black-white problem will forever fulfill our promise made by our founding fathers that "We hold these truths to be self-evident, that all Men are created equal, that they are endowed by their Creator with certain unalienable Rights, that among these are Life, Liberty and the Pursuit of Happiness."

2

Founding Grandfathers

Beginning American history with the landing of the pilgrims at Jamestown and Plymouth Rock ignores not only American Indians, but also the Spanish and the French. The first "Europeans" landing in the "New World" were African slaves abandoned by Spaniards in South Carolina in 1526. In 1562, the French Huguenots settled briefly in Florida and established their own fort there.

It is highly probable that the first non-native person to set foot in the new lands was a Spanish-speaking black man. And starting our history with the pilgrims, followed by the British and the American Revolution leaves out much we need to understand as to our black/white experience.

Before the beginning, there were the founding grandfathers. Our story originates in Europe at the end of the Middle Ages, or as it is sometimes called, "medieval times." The dates of this period is somewhat argumentative, depending on one's viewpoint; but I will deal with the period as if it occurred between the fall of the Roman Empire, 476 CE, to the discovery of the "New World" in 1492 CE.

After the fall of the Roman Empire, and the advent and growth of the Holy Roman Catholic Church, monarchism and feudalism was the norm in governing countries. This period in human history, contrary to many beliefs, was solid with human advancement with the introduction in the west of the Hindu-Arabic numbering system, the signing of the Magna Carta by King John, the founding of Golf, the invention of bottled beer and most importantly, at the end of the period, and probably the touchstone event that introduced the next period of human history; the invention of the Gutenberg printing press in 1455.

The next period of western human history has been called the "Enlightenment Period" or the "Age of Reason." No matter what it was called, both descriptions are accurate. It was the beginning of great thinking as to how mankind should live, how mankind should be governed and how mankind should conduct themselves in a just society.

No longer was the Catholic Church the last word on morality and philosophy (Author's disclaimer: I am Catholic), but men of science and philosophy began exchanging their ideas through the new mass media—the printed word.

From Nicholas Copernicus to Leonardo di Vinci, science, art and architecture flourished. The great thinkers and political philosophers of Europe would have a special relationship and contribution to the American experience. The Age of Reason was the catapault that invented the United States of America.

An understanding of Newton's Natural Laws promoted new thinking, unencumbered by trite thinking of the Church and the conventional beliefs of the times. Newton gave the men of the day permission to challenge conventional thinking, such as the "Rights of Kings" and methods of conducting commerce and government.

There was a boom in new political thinking, and with the new printing press spreading the new ideas over the landscape of Europe, things began to change very rapidly. Thinkers expressed their thoughts in writing and read the thoughts of others. The brilliant lights of the Enlightenment included the likes of Francis Bacon, Charles de Montesquieu, Voltaire, Jean Jacques Rosseau, David Hume, Adam Smith, and John Locke.

Our forefathers were products of this Enlightenment Age. Thomas Jefferson, John Jay, Benjamin Franklin, Alexander Hamilton, John Adams and James Madison all delivered masterpieces in the Declaration of Independence, which was inspired by John Locke, and the U. S. Constitution, which was inspired by the writings and works of Charles De Montesquieu.

It is Montesquieu who wrote about three branches of Government—the executive, legislative and judicial—and who wrote extensively about the separations of power and the role of laws in a just society. In his greatest work, "The Spirit of Laws Book," Montesquieu wrote about the institution of slavery. In Book XV, he wrote in Section 5 that:

> "*Were I to vindicate our right to make slaves of the negroes, these should be my arguments*":
>
> "The Europeans, having extirpated the Americans, were obliged to make slaves of the Africans, for clearing such vast tracts of land".

"Sugar would be too dear if the plants which produce it were cultivated by any other than slaves".

"These creatures are all over black, and with such a flat nose that they can scarcely be pitied".

"It is hardly to be believed that God, who is a wise Being, should place a soul, especially a good soul, in such a black ugly body".

"It is so natural to look upon colour as the criterion of human nature, that the Asiatics, among whom eunuchs are employed, always deprive the blacks of their resemblance to us by a more opprobrious distinction".

"The colour of the skin may be determined by that of the hair, which, among the Egyptians, the best philosophers in the world, was of such importance that they put to death all the red-haired men who fell into their hands.

"The negroes prefer a glass necklace to that of gold which polite nations so highly value. Can there be a greater proof of their wanting common sense?"

"It is impossible for us to suppose these creatures to be men, because, allowing them to be men, a suspicion would follow that we ourselves are not Christians."

"Weak minds exaggerate too much the wrong done to the Africans. For were the case as they state it, would the European powers, who make so many needless conventions among themselves, have failed to enter into a general one, in behalf of humanity and compassion?" [7]

Was this the dirty little secret that came over with the *Mayflower*? Was this their invisible cargo? Could this be America's Pandora's Box? Could this be the genesis of our black/white problem? Was this the catalyst to act or should it have been a caveat? Certainly a reading of our Constitution wherein blacks are counted as only three-fifths of a person underlies the rationale that our forefathers did not consider them whole humans. The Abolitionists of the 18th Century were devout Christians, including John Brown, and their Christian faith did not allow them to accept blacks as anything less than whole men, yearning to be free.

---

[7] Charles de Montesquieu. "The Spirit of Laws" Book XV, 1748

Our secular forefathers, Washington, Jefferson, Madison, each a slave owner, rationalized their behavior, not as Christians, but as enlightened men. Nevertheless, the most pervasive theme in our history is the domination of black America by white America. Race is the sharpest and deepest division in American life infinitely more than class distinction. Issues of black/white "relations propelled the Whig Party to collapse, prompted the formation of the Republican Party, and caused the Democratic Party to label itself the "white man's party" for almost a century."[8]

One of the few times Congress ever overrode a presidential veto was for the 1866 Civil Rights Act, passed by Republicans over the wishes of President Andrew Johnson. Southern Democratic Senators mounted the longest filibuster in U.S. History, more than 534 hours, to oppose the 1964 Civil Rights bill. Thomas Byrne Edsall has shown how race prompted the sweeping political realignment of 1964-1972, in which the white South went from a Democratic bastion to a Republican stronghold. "Race still affects American politics; George W. Bush won just 11 percent of the black vote, but won 57 percent of the white vote in 2004".[9]

We are what we were. Our forefathers wholeheartedly accepted the rationale of the "enlightened" men of Europe. As a result of their acceptance of their reason, the lot of black folks was codified in the U.S. constitution. As we shall learn, this codification and rationale protecting slavery led to the civil war, Jim Crow laws, and the oppressed existence of black Americans.

---

[8] James W. Loewen. "Lies my Teacher told me", A Touchstone Book, Simon and Schuster, New York, NY) Page 136.

[9] James W. Loewen. "Lies my Teacher told me," A Touchstone Book, Simon and Schuster, New York, NY Page 136

3

Creating A White Nation

Let us go back to yesteryear (One of the heroes of my youth was the Lone Ranger), and study the period right before the American Revolution to learn what got us here.

Every problem has a beginning and a root cause and to find it, you must dig deep and ask the tough questions of why. Why did the Colonists unite against Britain? Why did the Colonists reject the taxes imposed upon them by Britain? Why did Britain impose the "Intolerable Acts" upon the Colonists? Why did the Colonists unite and declare their independence from Britain and what did they want to be independent to do?

Freedom and Self-government? For what purpose?

Each of the thirteen original colonies was a charter (corporation) licensed by the King of England, responsible to him and subject to the kings laws. The leaders of the colonies could pass any law, enforce any law and conduct the business of the colonies in any way they wished, *as long as the laws were not in conflict with English Law!*

The colonies were not related to each other; each was a separate entity, like Coca Cola and Pepsi are today. They each ran their own enterprises, systems and laws, *as long as the enterprises, systems and laws were not in conflict with English Law!*

Each colony had a leader or leaders, all appointed by the King or elected by white male members of the colonies according to "the Rights of Englishmen." Colonial lawyers and judges were part of the "British Bench." Over 40 percent of the leaders of the thirteen chartered colonies were lawyers. In most cases, the lawyers were also farmers, land owners, land speculators and business men. There wasn't enough legal business to keep lawyers in business simply practicing law; however, their clients were also fellow farmers, land speculators and businessmen.

In almost all cases, the leaders of the southern colonies were slave owners. Slaves were property and were counted among the assets of the farmer-lawyer-planter. The first chartered colony was Virginia in 1609 and the last one was Georgia in 1739, so the thirteen original colonies had different histories, but all were subject to British law.

The "Glorious Revolution" of 1639 made English Parliament the key decision maker in English government, and it was the Parliament that called the tune as to the governance of the colonies. Life was not extraordinarily harsh for the colonies under these arrangements; however, there was always a feeling of "Damocles' Sword" hanging over the colonies. They never knew when England would impose her will on the colonies, and England did in various ways, most of which are familiar to American history students.

American history books make popular the events leading up to the American Revolution, including the Stamp Act of 1765, the Boston Massacre, and the Intolerable Acts. The Stamp Act made famous the bumper sticker slogan "No Taxation without Representation." The Boston Massacre of 1770 was a show of England's brute force when British soldiers killed five colonists, but the soldiers were subsequently acquitted by an American court. The British soldiers were ably represented by John Adams, who called the victims of the massacre nothing but "Negroes and mulatos, Irish teagues and outlandish Jacktars."[10] While important, these causes do not fully represent the basic fears and causes of our conflict with England.

There is little evidence of an increase in revolutionary furor among the colonies between 1770 and 1773, after the "massacre" although there were signs of discontent. The British accommodated the colonists by repealing some of the taxes imposed; however, there began an occupation of Boston and the sealing off of Boston Harbor after the Tea Party incident in 1773.

Tensions increased when Parliament passed the laws which became widely known in the colonies as the "Intolerable Acts," which greatly inhibited the colonists to govern their own colonies. It was these acts that began to bind the colonies together as each saw what could happen if England chose to clamp down. Included in the laws imposed by the British were the closing of Boston Harbor, the quartering of soldiers in folks' homes, the royal appointments of local leadership, trial of British officials only by Englishmen in England, and the most outlandish of the acts, the recognition of Roman Catholic rights in Canada as equal to American rights.

---

[10] Alfred W. & Ruth Blumrosen. "Slave Nation, How Slavery United the Colonies & Sparked the American Revolution." Sourcebooks, Inc. Naperville, Illinois 2005. page 20

The Intolerable Acts were meant to punish the colonists and to bring to their attention British might and British rule. The unintended consequences of the acts were the binding of the colonies against a common enemy. But were these acts enough to bring about the American Revolution?

The underlying factor that the acts manifested was that the British, whenever it chose, could impose its will on the colonies by use of force and intimidation. What else could the British do more than what it has already done? One of the things the British could have done was tax slaves as property; however, the colonists knew this was not probable. So what was?

A well publicized outcome of a trial in England of the slave James Somerset in 1772 was the singular event that struck fear in the hearts of American leaders. The James Somerset case was almost an exact replica of a future Dred Scott case in America in 1857, but with a different outcome.

James Somerset, an American black slave, sued for his freedom as an escaped slave in England. When he won his case in a Court of Kings Bench and became a free man, the case also closed slavery forever in England in 1772. There was such a celebration in England among the black population, and white simpaticos that it was widely covered in all the newspapers, and much of that news came to the American colonies.

The King's Bench was the oldest and highest common law court in England; it was so named because in earlier years, the king himself sat in judgment in that court. In 1772, it consisted of a chief justice and four associate justices. One was William Blackstone, the author of the *Commentaries on the Law of England*, which were well known to colonial lawyers. In 1765, he had written his interpretations of the confused English precedents concerning slavery:

> "And this spirit of liberty, is so deeply implanted in our constitution, and rooted even in our very soil, that a slave or a Negro, the moment he lands in England, falls under the protection of the laws and so far becomes a freeman".[11]

England had shown with the Intolerable Acts that they could pass laws without consultation, so the colonist's petitioned Parliament to end slave trade, but not slavery, as its commerce could not sustain such a shock. It was highly probable that the English parliament would have eliminated slavery in a very short time.

---

[11] Slave Nation, ibid. page 6

In the minds of the colonists, especially the most influential Virginia colony, the die was cast. Slavery could be ended by fiat!

It would not be inaccurate to state that the American Revolution was to free white men, to enslave black people, and to carry out its business without outside interference.

It would not be inaccurate to state that the fight for Texas independence from Mexico in 1835, was for exactly the same reasons; the right to enslave black people for commercial purposes.

And it would most certainly be accurate to state that the American Civil War, 1860 to 1865, was to eliminate slavery for all time in the United States of America.

> "Somerset never knew that his private quest for freedom was the spark that helped start the American Revolution and that has haunted the nation down to the present day." [12]

> *"We hold these truths to be self-evident, that all men are created equal . . . ."*

These words beginning the second paragraph of the Declaration of Independence are among the most powerful words ever written by civilized man; however, the men who authored them were better preachers than practitioners. They didn't intend for their words to apply to *all men.*

The Declaration of Independence did not apply to black people living in America; therefore, I do not use the term "black Americans," or "African-Americans," because they were not American citizens until July 9, 1865 with the ratification of the Fourteenth Amendment to the Constitution.

Most folks in America are acquainted with the "I Have a Dream" speech by Martin Luther King delivered on August 28, 1963 on the steps of the Lincoln Memorial in Washington, D.C . . . . Following are excerpts from that speech.

> *"In a sense we've come to our nation's capital to cash a check. When the architects of our republic wrote the magnificent words of the Constitution and the Declaration of Independence, they were signing a promissory note to which every American was to fall heir. This note was a promise that all men, yes, black men as well as white men, would be guaranteed the unalienable rights of life, liberty and the pursuit of happiness. It is obvious today that America has defaulted on this promissory note, insofar as her citizens of color are concerned. Instead of honoring this sacred*

---

[12] Slave Nation, ibid. page 14.

> obligation, America has given the Negro people a bad check, a check which has come back marked 'insufficient funds.'"
>
> "I have a dream that one day this nation will rise up and live out the true meaning of its creed: 'We hold these truths to be self-evident, that all men are created equal.'"

Dr. King was not accurate when he alluded that America had defaulted on the promissory note because the Declaration of Independence was never intended to apply to "negroes." From the inception of the republic, blacks have been shut out and systems were put in place across the United States—North, South, East and West—assuring that blacks would remain at the bottom of the socio-economic ladder in the United States. For hundreds of years, there has been a concerted effort by government and society to specifically prevent blacks from achieving their potential as human beings and contributors to American society.

Our forefathers had plenty of opportunities to include blacks in their plan for an American Republic and history surely indicates that the "peculiar institution" of slavery was discussed thoroughly by the authors of the Declaration of Independence and the authors of the Constitution. They decided to do nothing and to leave the problem to future generations.

Winston Churchill, in his famous *Iron Curtain* speech in 1946 said about World War II: *"there never was a war in history easier to prevent by timely action than the one which has just desolated such great areas of the globe . . . It could have been prevented in my belief without the firing of a single shot, but no one would listen and one by one we were all sucked into the awful whirlpool."*

The same could be said about the American Civil War if they had taken care of our black and white problem from the inception of the republic and writing of the U.S. Constitution.

Blacks were specifically recognized in the U.S. Constitution as representing three-fifths of a person in determining the number of representatives states could send to Congress, although all blacks currently residing in the colonies were not slaves. They were counted but not recognized as human persons with certain *unalienable rights . . .*

It has always puzzled me that if the black man was inferior, why was it a necessity to legislate that fact? If whites were superior, wasn't it obvious that they would always be the victor in any fair competition, whether in sports or business or academia, when in direct competition with the black man?

White superiority was a legal position, established for dominance, and not a literal one as recognized by Thomas Jefferson. In a letter to Benjamin Banneker, black man and son of slaves, who was the surveyor of the newly developed Federal District, which is now Washington, D.C, Jefferson wrote on August 30, 1791:

> *Nobody wishes more than I do to see such proofs as you exhibit, that nature has given to our black brethren, talents equal to those of the other colors of men, & that the appearance of a want of them is owing merely to the degraded conditions of their existence both in Africa & America I can add with truth that nobody wishes more ardently to see a good system commenced for raising the condition both of their body & mind to what it ought to be, as fast as the imbecility of the present existence, and other circumstances which cannot be neglected, will admit . . .* [13]

Thomas Jefferson certainly was aware of the potential talent of Negroes if educated and conditions were such that they could experience everything the same as whites. Education was important to Mr. Jefferson and he took great pride *in authoring "a system of general instruction, which shall reach every description of our citizens, from the richest to the poorest, as it was the earliest so will it be the latest of all the public concerns in which I shall permit myself to take an interest."*[14]

> *"I accordingly prepared three bills for the Revisal, proposing three distinct grades of education, reaching all classes: 1. Elementary school for all children generally, rich and poor. 2. Colleges for a middle degree of instruction, calculated for the common purposes of life, and such as would be desirable for all who are in easy circumstances. And 3. An ultimate grade for teaching the sciences generally and in their highest degree".*[15]

> *"If the condition of man is to be progressively ameliorated, as we fondly hope & believe, education is to be the chief instrument in affecting it."*[16]

Unfortunately, the enlightened Mr. Jefferson's theories and practices on education and knowledge did not apply to Africans living in America. Much has been written that Thomas Jefferson was a benevolent slave owner and did teach trades and many of his chattels learned to read and write; however, they remained slaves. Much has been written that it was just the way it was, and granting slaves their "unalienable rights" would not be a practical thing to do.

---

[13] "The Quotable Jefferson," page 351. Princeton University Press, John Kaminski, Princeton, NJ

[14] *"The Quotable Jefferson"*, ibid. page 86]

[15] "The Quotable Jefferson", ibid. pg 86]

[16] "The Quotable Jefferson," ibid. pg. 87]

Benjamin Franklin, the Founding Father who was the most pragmatic and less ideological than his contemporaries, founded an organization in 1750 that established a school for black children in Philadelphia, Pennsylvania. In 1753, three years after the school was established, Franklin visited the school and observed:

> "I was on the whole much pleased, and what I then saw have conceived a higher opinion of natural capacities of the black race than I had ever before entertained. Their apprehension seems as quick, their memory as strong, and their docility in every respect equal to that of white children. You will wonder perhaps that I should ever doubt it, and I will not undertake to justify all my prejudices."[17]

The observations of Benjamin Franklin were made 23 years before the Declaration of Independence and 34 years before the adoption of the U.S. Constitution.

There is a wonderful book, *"The First Emancipator, The Forgotten Story of Robert Carter, The Founding Father Who Freed His Slaves"* by Andrew Levy. Robert Carter was neighbor and kin to the Washington and Lees and a friend and peer to Thomas Jefferson and George Mason. On September 15, 1791, Robert Carter executed a document he called his "Deed of Gift" that granted freedom to his nearly 500 slaves, the largest single act of liberation in the history of American slavery before the Emancipation Proclamation.

The Father of our Country, George Washington, owner of 500 slaves, and the Marquis de Lafayette had planned to develop a large estate together in Virginia totally absent of slaves, but their plans went unfulfilled because of the pending revolution in France.

So if our founding fathers recognized that blacks had the potential to learn, if educated, and there were examples among the elite gentry of emancipating slaves, why didn't they do it? Because educating black folks and setting them free was not good business.

Large landowners believed they could not compete without cheap labor and could not trust their neighbor to "let their people go" if they let their own go!

A case in point illustrating achievement among early blacks living in America is the story of one, James Forten. *Young James Forten was a boy of 10 when the Revolutionary War broke out in his native Philadelphia in 1777. The young Forten, second generation of his*

---

[17] Walter Isaacson. Benjamin Franklin, An American Life. Simon & Schuster Paperbacks, New York, NY. Page 153

family born free in America, marched off proudly as a drummer boy with the local militia who, like him, thought they were fighting for their homes and liberty against the British invasion.

> *When James Forten was born in 1767, there were slaves working plantations in the Philadelphia area and serving in the households of prosperous Americans like Benjamin Franklin. But more and more moral pressure was being brought to bear by Quaker reformers. In 1750, Anthony Benezet, a Quaker schoolteacher of French Huguenot descent whose family had fled persecution in France, opened a free evening school for black children in his own home. Benezet's writings against slavery reached London, where his pamphlets influenced humanitarians such as William Wilberforce and Granville Sharp to roll up their sleeves and work to abolish slavery. By 1770, Quaker societies in England and Philadelphia raised the money for a school building for free black children. James Forten enrolled at age 8 in 1775, at the time of the Second Continental Congress and remained there until he followed the local militia as their drummer boy.*
>
> *On July 31, 1781, taking a chest of clothes, his bible, and a bag of marbles, James Forten, along with nineteen other black recruits, joined the Navy, James serving as a powder boy during battle and as a cabin boy when not.*
>
> *James Forten's luck did not last. While serving on the USS Royal Louis, was captured by the British and he now faced a fate worse than he ever imagined. Under the international rules of war, blacks captured on the high seas were treated not as prisoners of war, but as their captors booty; they were usually sold into slavery to work for the rest of their lives on the Caribbean sugar plantations.*
>
> *And herein come the importance of the marbles. The young son of the British captain spotted James playing marbles and asked to play with him. The two young chaps became friends and the Captain's son asked his father to spare young James Forten so he would have a play companion. Having all the authority of a British Naval Captain, the Captain gave James and the other black prisoners the choice of joining the Royal Navy or being held as prisoners of war until the war ended.*
>
> *Young James Forten declined the first option: "I am here as a prisoner for the liberties of my country. I cannot prove a traitor to her interests."*[18]

Unfortunately, the America that young James Forten pledged allegiance to did not reciprocate.

---

[18] William Stearn Randall & Nancy Nahra. "Forgotten Americans", Barnes & Noble, NY, NY. Page 150.

Over time slave owners, and those who benefited from slave labor, rationalized their actions through religion, by dehumanizing black people, and through fear of miscegenation of blacks with whites. Interracial marriage and interracial sex was prohibited by law in the Thirteen Original Colonies from the seventeenth century onwards and subsequently in several U.S. States until 1967 when the Supreme Court ruled on Loving v. Virginia.

One wonders where all the "mulatto" children came from.

America, in the 18th and 19th Centuries, profited from slave labor and that profit has never been shared with America's black citizens.

Education was the foundation of our growth as a nation and typically the youth of the 18th and early 19th centuries learned through an ever expanding public school system. By the late 1840's, a typical curriculum for a grade school student included classes in Latin, Greek, Italian, mathematics, elocution and public speaking, debate, and in most cases, religion.

In the very best schools, there was a diverse student body, as the elite from foreign countries would send their children to American's best boarding schools. Typically at Boston's Latin School were students from Italy, Greece, Turkey, Columbia, Cuba, Canada, Brazil, England and the southern states. Blacks living in America did not attend as they were not permitted to receive any education.

The very best students, and those who could afford to go, went on to Harvard, Yale, Princeton and Amherst Colleges. The establishment of America's elite was well on its way and obviously, no blacks were admitted to America's elite universities until the 20th century, and that was for a very limited number.

A free public education became a popular experience for white America in the mid 19th century and public education became law in most states by the beginning of the 20th century, but especially in the New England states did education flourish. The southern states were a different matter.

The race is not always won by the fastest man, but the educated man definitely has a better chance at success in our country.

4

Dredful Dred Scott

In my 20's and 30's, I proudly belonged to my town's Jaycees, Junior Chamber of Commerce, where we recited the Jaycee Creed with enthusiasm and belief. ". . . . *That government should be of laws rather than of men."* Despite this truth, Supreme Court cases, such as Dred Scott (1857), Plessey v. Ferguson (1896) and other 19th and 20th century cases, tell a different reality—that we are a nation of laws interpreted by men, given their times, biases and circumstances. The aforementioned pivotal cases concern the 14th Amendment, which ensures the rights of citizens under the law, including due process.

The touchstone event in American history that forevermore divided America was the infamous Dred Scott Decision. Dred Scott, an African slave living in America, was taken by his master from the slave state of Missouri to the free state of Illinois and then to the free territory of Wisconsin, where he lived for a long time.

When the Army ordered his master to go back to Missouri, Scott voluntarily followed him back to that slave state, along with a newly acquired wife and two children. Dr. John Emerson, the army officer who owned Scott, died in 1846. Soon thereafter, Scott attempted to purchase his freedom for himself and his family from Emerson's widow, Irene. After his offer was rejected, Scott initiated a lawsuit against Mrs. Emerson to win his freedom.[19]

Scott's opinion was that when Dr. Emerson had taken him, and his family, to Fort Armstrong, Illinois, a Free State, he was emancipated by default. When the army surgeon moved with Scott to Fort Snelling, which was designated free territory under the terms of the 1854 Missouri Compromise, Emerson had by default, changed Scott's legal status from slave to free black. Previous Missouri Supreme Court decisions supported Scott's claim. "In those decisions, the state's highest court had

---

[19] James F. Simon. "Lincoln and Chief Justice Taney", Simon & "Schuster Paperbacks, New York, London, Sydney, PG. 100

ruled that once a slave had left Missouri to reside in a Free State or territory, he became free. Scott lost the first trial on a technicality, but won his case in a second trial on precisely those grounds."[20]

Irene Emerson, appealed the case to the Missouri Supreme Court, where circumstances had changed since the court had ruled in Scott's favor. What had changed? Missouri was trying to figure out what it was going to be. A Free State or a Slave State, and along with Kansas, experienced some of the bloodiest events prior to the Civil War. Tensions were hot and it was the period when John Brown, an abolitionist, killed five white slave sympathizers in what was known as the Pottawatomie Massacre.

Attitudes were different than during the prior ruling. "The respect extended by Missouri to the laws of Free states, under the doctrine of comity, disappeared, replaced by a militant defense of slavery."[21]

By reversing Dred Scott's earlier court victory, the Missouri Supreme Court reflected the anger that Missouri possessed against free-states—in other words it wasn't a nation of laws, but a state of angry men. Therefore, the Missouri Supreme Court rejected the argument that Missouri was obligated to recognize the laws of the free state of Illinois because another state had no right to tell them how to run their affairs. The Missouri court also dismissed federal law theory that Dred Scott was a free man as a result of the Compromise of 1820 that prohibited slavery in the Louisiana Territory. In reality, Missouri affirmed they owed allegiance to Missouri law only. In their eyes, Dred Scott should remain a slave and he belonged to Irene Emerson.

Recognizing that earlier decisions of his court had come to the opposite conclusion, Judge William Scott suggested that those decisions had come about during a period of relative tranquility between North and South. A new vigilance in the slave states was now necessary, said Judge Scott. Having lost in the Missouri Supreme Court, Dred Scott appealed his case to the United States Supreme Court in 1856.

The Chief Justice of the United States Supreme Court was Roger Taney, a former slave owner from Maryland, an avowed southern sympathizer and states rights advocate, was appointed by President Andrew Jackson in 1836. In future years, Taney would thwart the efforts of Abraham Lincoln in opposing the suspension of Habeas Corpus by Lincoln during a time of insurrection. He also led the opposition as chief justice in opposing the war time draft of Union soldiers and opposed the

---

[20] "Lincoln and Chief Justice Taney", ibid, pg. 101
[21] "Lincoln and Chief Justice Taney", Page 101.

monetary strategies of the Lincoln administration during the war. In almost each decision, Taney ruled against the Union and in favor of the Confederate cause.

In writing the decision concerning Dred Scott, Chief Justice Taney was consistent in his belief of the sovereignty of the states over the federal government as regards to "property." The Dred Scott decision was truly an interpretation made by men—five of the seven justices were southerners—and not by a clear interpretation of law, and the intent of Congress.

At the time of the Dred Scott decision, there were 4 million black people in America, which included over 3.6 million slaves, almost all living in the South.

The decision impacted all black people, slave or free, living in the United States, meaning that black folks living in the Northeast of the United States who were citizens, and had been voting since the inception of the Republic, could no longer vote and were now aliens in their birth land.

What was the true impact of the Dred Scott decision to today's black population? As the white population continued to advance in education, commerce, industry and property ownership, free blacks were set back "prior to 1776" and black slaves, were denied all hope of ever rising beyond their lot. White America was living in 1857 while blacks were living in the America of 1775.

The Taney Court also nullified the Missouri Compromise of 1820, which prohibited slavery north of the "Mason/Dixon line. Taney said that the Missouri Compromise deprived white men of their rights to property without due process of law.

Abolitionists cited the Dred Scott ruling as evidence that the South was aggressively wanting to expand slavery throughout the new American nation. Southerners cited the ruling as a victory of States Rights and as a victory for their way of life.

Private citizen and political activist, Abraham Lincoln, was so angered by the Dred Scott decision that he made a personal commitment to involve himself in the national debate, catapulting him to fame when he debated Steven Douglas seven times in 1858.

An excerpt from the majority opinion, written by Roger Taney, stated:

> *"We think they [people of African ancestry] are not citizens, and that they are not included, and were not intended to be included, under the word "citizens" in the Constitution, and can therefore claim none of the rights and privileges which that instrument provides for and secures to citizens of the United States.*

> *The legislation and histories of the times, and the language used in the Declaration of Independence, show, that neither the class of persons who had been imported as slaves, nor their descendants, whether they had become free or not, were then acknowledged as a part of the people, nor intended to be included in the general words used in that memorable instrument:*

The Supreme Court decision was devastating. Not only did they throw out Dred Scott's case, they ruled that slaves had no right to bring legal action and that the U.S. Constitution and the Bill of Rights did not apply to Africans living in America. The Missouri Compromise was also declared unconstitutional, and that Congress had no authority to limit slavery in the territories. Chief Justice Roger Taney put it as bluntly as he could: blacks were "so far inferior that they had no rights which the white man was bound to respect."[22]

The Dred Scott decision, in the joyful words of one Georgia newspaper, "covers every question regarding slavery and settles it in favor of the South . . . A slave was a slave, whether in Massachusetts or South Carolina. The Supreme Court had officially declared slavery a national institution."

The opposition was devastated. "They have sown the wind", warned Henry Ward Beecher, an important American preacher, "and they will reap the whirlwind."[23]

America had never been as divided as in 1859. For ten years, the slavocracy had won one symbolic victory after another for "Southern Rights," but to their chagrin each victory only brought more resistance from the North without adding one square mile of actual slave territory. After years of antagonism, southern spokesmen had shifted from a reluctant defense to a defiant celebration of slavery and a loathing of all things Yankee. As the Richmond Examiner wrote:

> *We have got to hating everything with the prefix free, from free negroes down and up through the whole catalogue—free farms, free labor, free society, free will, free thinking, free children, and free schools—all belonging to the same brood of damnable isms. But the worst of all abominations is the modern system of free schools, which has been the cause and prolific source of the infidelity and treasons*

---

[22] Debby Applegate. "The Most Famous Man in America", The Biography of Henry Ward Beecher". Page 288. Doubleday Books, Randon House, NY, NY.

[23] The Most Famous Man in America", The Biography of Henry Ward Beecher". Page 288. Debby Applegate, Doubleday Books, Randon House, NY, NY.

> *that have turned the [Northern] cities into Sodoms and Gomorrahs, and her land into the nestling places of howling Bedlamites.*[24]

Where did the hatred and condescension towards blacks come from that it had to be codified into our laws? We are who we were, and what we were before we were Americans, was English.

The early legal profession in the United States was educated in English Common law and most legal books were those written by Sir William Blackstone. The academic works of Blackstone was an early influence on our American legal system and he had the same impact on our legal profession as Locke or Montesquieu had on our politicians.

Blackstone's most famous work was his *Commentaries on the Laws of England* (1803) and his influence and theories were cited in the early Supreme Court decisions by the United States at least ten to twelve times a year.

The works of William Blackstone were the only law library used by the United States legal system for almost the first century of its existence. Among American lawyers who were influenced by Blackstone included John Jay, first Chief Justice of the Supreme Court, John Adams, John Marshall, 4th Chief Justice and later, Abraham Lincoln.

What did this most influential legal mind say about "negroes?"

From Blackstone's Commentaries on the Laws of England (1803), p. 44 and quoted by St. George Tucker:

> "*Let no Negroe or mulattoe be capable of taking, holding or exercising any public office, freehold, franchise or privilege . . . Nor of keeping or bearing arms, unless authorized to do by some act of the general assembly, whose duration shall be limited to three years.*"

Certainly if it was good enough for Blackstone, it was good enough for our forefathers.

It is an irony, that in the case of Dred Scott, if the United States had not separated herself from England in 1776, Dred Scott would have been a free man in 1833, albeit an Englishman, but a free man.

The English Parliament passed their Slavery Abolition Act in August of 1833, after years of debate led by William Wilberforce, and without a shot being fired. The slave

---

[24] "The Most Famous Man in America", ibid. page 306

trade and slavery, forevermore, was forbidden in every English colony throughout the world. However, it is important to note, that although, slavery was abolished, Negroes were not given equal citizenship status nor were they considered "equal to an Englishman."

A further irony was that Mrs. Emerson, the widow, remarried during the trial of Dred Scott to an abolitionist. When Scott was returned to Mrs. Emerson as a slave, her new husband returned him and his family to his original owners, the Blow family, in Missouri.

The Blow family were also Missouri abolitionists and immediately freed Scott and his family. Three months after the Supreme Court ruling, Dred Scott died of pneumonia, a free man.

A footnote to this history and the parliamentary heroics of William Wilberforce, the first American University owned and operated by African Americans is Wilberforce University located in Wilberforce, Ohio. The university was founded in 1856 and named in honor of the 18th century English statesman and abolitionist.

5

Civil War Plus

The Republican Party was founded in 1854 on a single principle—the non extension of slavery—and the first major political party in America to have no southern wing at all. It declared itself a "party of principle and modern Christian morality."

In 1860, the republicans elected Abraham Lincoln as their candidate for President.

Abraham Lincoln, the Great Emancipator, had the following to say during the fourth Lincoln-Douglas debate of 1858:

> *"I will say then that I am not, nor ever have been in favor of bringing about in anyway the social and political equality of the white and black races—that I am not nor ever have been in favor of making voters or jurors of negroes, nor of qualifying them to hold office, nor to intermarry with white people; and I will say in addition that there is a physical difference between the white and black races which I believe will forever forbid the two races living together on terms of social and political equality. And inasmuch as they cannot so live, while they do remain together there must be the position of superior and inferior and I as much as any other man am in favor of having the superior position assigned to the white race. I say upon this occasion I do not perceive that because the white man is to have the superior position the negro should be denied everything."*

I love Abraham Lincoln, but he was a man of his time and his beliefs were his reality and his reality was the norm of many of his white contemporaries and they acted on their beliefs by prohibiting negroes from intermarrying, voting, owning property, serving as a juror and being forbidden to act as a witness in jury trials, even as a witness in his own defense.

Remember that Abraham Lincoln was not an abolitionist. His main goal as President was to preserve the Union and he explored as many means possible to accomplish this goal. We are not going into great detail here, but there were many citizens of the

United States, tried and true Abolitionists, who believed that the Negro was a whole man, one of God's children, and should have all the rights accorded all men.

The socially accepted body of beliefs that framed Lincoln's thinking did not disappear in the 19th century and were not uncommon among other distinguished Presidents in the 20th century that I will comment on in a later chapter. One example, however, was President Richard Nixon, who in a recorded taped conversation said that one of the only reasons that he could support abortion is if the child to be born was one of black and white union.

But Father Abe evolved. As Jefferson discovered with Banneker, Lincoln's attitudes shifted upon meeting Frederick Douglass, a self-educated former slave. On January 1, 1863, Abraham Lincoln issued an Executive Order proclaiming that all slaves, currently held by states in rebellion against the United States, would be set free. The Emancipation Proclamation did not free all slaves as those living in states and territories "not in conflict with the United States" were not set free. Kentucky, Missouri, Delaware, and West Virginia were border states in league with the Union, for the most part, in fighting against the rebellion.

During Lincoln's campaign for President for a second term, he urged Congress to pass a constitutional amendment abolishing slavery forever throughout the United States and after he was reelected, he successfully convinced Congress to pass the Thirteenth Amendment to the U.S. Constitution. The Thirteenth Amendment banned slavery in all the U.S. states and territories, and was ratified by enough states to become law by December 6, 1865, nearly 7 months after Abraham Lincoln was assassinated.

Peace was at hand, and slavery was abolished, but now what? Could negroes vote? Were they citizens of the United States? The answer to both those questions was a resounding no.

The legacy of the Civil War was the abolishment of slavery and the authority of the national government over the state governments. At the end of the Civil War, two questions hung over the political landscape. What would happen to the former rebel states? What would happen to the former slaves? The assassination of Abraham Lincoln brought forward Andrew Johnson as President of the United States. Johnson, a southern Democrat, was quoted more than once that "This is a country for white men and, by God, as long as I am President it shall be governed for white men."

Johnson's pugnacious attitude towards blacks was a long way from Abraham Lincoln's last great speech in his second inaugural address—"With malice toward none, with charity for all," and Lincoln's vision of a "new birth of freedom."

In 1870, there were 4.8 million black people living in the United States and of those, 4.4 million were living in the former Confederate States of America. Would the Reconstruction Era in the south add value to the lives of freed slaves? There is historical evidence that the answer was yes.

There is overwhelming evidence that former slaves grabbed hold of freedom after the Civil War by securing their families, improving their education, and seeking and wielding political power. This political power, such as holding elected office and voting, was accompanied by economic strength and personal independence. Political power was the key as without it, control of life in commerce, education and access to the legal system was non-existent.

From the moment of liberation, most former slaves saw freedom in traditional terms; they focused on building strong families, obtaining property and accumulating wealth. They expressed the republican virtues of the founding fathers themselves as they set out to balance self-interest with the well being of local communities. [25]

Central to the African American definition of liberty was religious freedom. The African American churches advocated civil society and community activism. It provided a meeting place, solidified community spirit, and often focused activism toward social and political ends. A source of strength for black leaders, the church inspired the application of ethics to the political problems of the postwar period. Through Christian doctrine, black culture preached reconciliation rather than revenge as a reaction to past bondage.

Slaves accepted Christianity quite easily as they saw in this religion hope in the afterlife from the "hell" they were living on earth. They attended church services regularly and found relief, friendship and camaraderie in the early churches of their communities. After the Civil War, in the months after Appomattox, the new black communities used whatever building was available, to gather for their worship, and for their education. Volunteers from northern communities used the churches as classrooms to begin educating the heretofore illiterate population of former black slaves.

The story of Robert Smalls needs telling: Robert Smalls, born around 1839 in South Carolina, near where the South fired the first shot of the Civil War. Circumstances brought Robert Smalls and the Civil War together. Smalls had been working during his young life as a pilot in the port of Charleston, South Carolina and was assigned to do pilot work when war broke out between North and South.

---

[25] Orville Vernon Burton. "The Age of Lincoln," Hill & Wang, A Division of Farrar, Straus & Dixon. New York, NY. Page 252

One evening, as he sat at the helm of a Confederate transport, the Captain and officers of the ship went ashore, leaving young Smalls alone in the Captains tower. The ship was being manned by other black slaves and they decided to hijack the ship and escape to the north to become free men.

Robert Smalls and his crew made a daring sea escape. He and the others managed to get by five confederate ships guarding the harbor, and slip under the noses of the guards at Fort Sumter. He and his five slave brethren, made it to the Union fleet, which had been sitting outside the harbor forming a blockade.

Smalls was enlisted in the Union Navy, and became America's first black Naval Captain. During his youth in South Carolina, Smalls taught himself to read and write and after the Civil War, put his leadership skills and influence to better the lot of his fellow free men. He became a property owner in South Carolina and donated land for a school to which freedmen came "at all hours . . . expecting to catch a lesson."[26]

During Reconstruction, Robert Smalls became a Congressman representing South Carolina and served three separate terms. During consideration of a bill to reduce and restructure the United States Army he introduced an amendment that included this wording, "Hereafter in the enlistment of men in the Army . . . no distinction whatsoever shall be made on account of race or color." The amendment was not considered. Another great opportunity lost.

The vast majority of freed African Americans saw educational opportunity as integral to freedom, part and parcel of their determination "never to be made slaves again."[27] Whites did whatever it took to prevent the education of former slaves; however, there were considerable free educated blacks from the "north" and northern whites who came south to educate the former slaves, some at the peril of their own lives.

Teachers were threatened and some killed. Churches, which also housed schools, were burned. But despite this, it did not halt the deep thirst for education in African American communities. Each gain proved cumulative: from basic literacy and elementary arithmetic, freed people mounted upward. Among the hundreds of secondary schools and colleges founded during Reconstruction were Fisk in Nashville, Tennessee (1866) and the Augusta Institute in Georgia (1867), the latter

---

[26] I could not find a reference for this quote.but I liked it so much that I use it with apologies to the one who said it first. aim

[27] "The Age of Lincoln", Orville Vernon Burton, page 254. Hill & Wang, A Division of Farrar, Straus & Dixon. New York, NY.

moving to Atlanta onto land donated by fellow Baptist John D. Rockefeller, the college was subsequently renamed Morehouse College.[28]

Despite acts of violence and arson committed against churches and schoolhouses, African Americans persisted and made progress in educating their children and reducing illiteracy. In 1860, only about 10 percent of the adult African American population could read; by 1870, that figure increased to 30 percent. In 1900, it had risen to 55.5 percent. Poor whites were concerned that freedmen would surpass them in literacy, but that never happened; white literacy rates remained at about 80 percent. Louisiana saw a decrease in white literacy when it quit funding education at the end of Reconstruction.[29]

---

[28] Orville Vernon Burton. "The Age of Lincoln. Hill & Wang, A Division of Farrar, Straus & Dixon. New York, NY. Page 255

[29] Orville V. Burton. "The Age of Lincoln," Hill & Wang, A Division of Farrar, Straus & Dixon. New York, NY. Page 255

6

Forty Acres And A Mule

Real freedom, as classical republican ideology understood it and religious expectation framed it, required autonomy in an agriculture economy that meant living off one's own land. For centuries, black Americans had been told they did not belong: owning land proved they did. Surely the "Day of Jubilee" that Mr. Lincoln's armies had brought on must entail an act of retribution toward the master class, at least the transfer of "forty acres and a mule" as tokens of redress.

On January 16, 1865, with the approval of Abraham Lincoln, General William Tecumseh Sherman, The Commander of the West, issued Special Order No. 15 which subdivided hundreds of thousands of acres of farmland along the South Carolina and Georgia coast "so that each family shall have a plot of not more than forty acres of tillable ground." The experiment was successful. Within six months, more than forty thousand freedmen were farming land they thought was theirs to keep.[30]

On April 15, 1865 Abraham Lincoln died of wounds from the assassin John Wilkes Booth. Andrew Johnson, Lincoln's Vice President, succeeded him, who among many other deeds, rescinded the "forty acres and a mule" order in August of 1865. "Conservatives in Congress also opposed distribution of confiscated Confederate land to the freedmen as a threat to private property."[31]

In contrast during this same period, the U.S. Government did offer immense land grants and gave direct aid to the railroad industry in amounts unheard of in this nation. There were no objections in Congress or in the general public as much of the acreage of the West was forked over to the railroads.

---

[30] Vernon Burton. "The Age of Lincoln," Orville Hill & Wang, A Division of Farrar, Straus & Dixon. New York, NY. page 259.

[31] Orville Vernon Burton, "The Age of Lincoln," Hill & Wang, A Division of Farrar, Straus & Dixon. New York, NY.

The largest employer in the American West was the U.S. Government with military forces assisting settlers in "taming the west" and assisting in the construction of the railroad industry. There were over 100 military forts in the Western United States, not to fend off Indian raids, but to assist settlers, miners and ranchers to settle the West.

Some familiar places were Fort Leavenworth, Fort Scott, Fort Dodge, Fort Riley, and Fort Hays in Kansas. New Mexico had Fort Bayard, Fort Craig, Fort Selden and many others. Arizona had Fort Defiance, Fort Apache, Fort Huachuca among others and Texas had numerous forts such as Fort Dodge, and Fort Worth. Wyoming, Colorado and California had numerous forts such as Fort Laramie, Fort Collins, and Fortress Alcatraz, respectively. Nebraska also had a Fort Laramie.

The "Little House on the Prairie" was fully protected by America's might. There were no forts specifically established to protect the interests of millions of black people.

Just as mythical as the pejorative Reconstruction Period is the myth that every white person in the South was against the former slaves. Even prior to the Civil War and during the war, many southerners remained loyal to the concept of Union. They were anti-secessionists and were in disagreement with the southern aristocrats.

A Mississippi widow, in filing a claim for wartime misfortune wrote, "*My Grandfather was killed in the Revolutionary War. My brother was with Jackson at New Orleans and I had nephews in the Mexican War and nephews in the late war in the Union Army. I believed in Gen'l Jackson and did not think it was right to destroy what he had saved.*"

Her neighbor said, "*I never believed in the war of Jeff Davis I always believed in the United States Government I did not believe in secession . . . had I had the chance I would have shot Jeff Davis.*"[32]

During Reconstruction, southern whites who joined the Republican Party were called *scalawags*. *Scalawags* formed a coalition with northern newcomers, called *Carpetbaggers* and *Freedmen*, blacks who were former slaves. The terms were pejorative and used by hostile Democrats during Reconstruction after the war.

Some of the most prominent *scalawags* were General James Longstreet, Robert E. Lee's top general; Joseph E. Brown, the wartime Governor of Georgia; and James Lusk Alcorn of Mississippi, the founder of Alcorn State University in 1871. Another famous *scalawag* was Samuel L. Phillips, the lawyer who argued against segregation in Plessy vs. Ferguson (1896).

---

[32] Orville Vernon Burton. "The Age of Lincoln," Hill & Wang, A Division of Farrar, Straus & Dixon. New York, NY. Page 247.

Scalawags should not be a derogatory term! Unfortunately, over time, our overly sensitized view of the "mistreated South" had made *Scalawag* and *Carpetbagger* derogatory words.

The Union always had supporters in the South. The mountain districts of Appalachia, eastern Kentucky and Tennessee, the mountains of North Carolina and the Ozarks of Arkansas were Republican, or Scalawag, strongholds and did not support the politicians who dominated the Confederacy.

They were mostly poor folk, committed to their families, and not to the southern cause. They were not slave holders and were not beholden to "cheap cotton." Andrew Jackson, 7th President of the United States and first president to be born west of the Appalachians was their representative leader. They welcomed the reconstruction of the New South and supported what the Radical Republicans were trying to do in the southern communities.

The Reconstruction of the south began under President Andrew Johnson, who almost immediately offered blanket amnesty to all but the very highest-level rebel leaders and ordered all land in federal hands returned to its former owners, evicting the freed blacks who'd settled on them which sparked a series of violent confrontations in the South.

Johnson gave each state free rein to begin reconstituting their governments, requiring only that they repudiate secession, abolish slavery and forfeit all Confederate debts.[33]

The moderate policies of Andrew Johnson towards the Southern states infuriated radical Republicans who attempted to remove him from office. Although he was impeached, he was not removed from office and remained there until replaced in the following presidential election.

The Fourteenth Amendment to the U. S. Constitution was ratified on July 9, 1868 on Johnson's watch and gave "to all persons born or naturalized in the United States . . . to be citizens of the United States." The question of citizenship was resolved for Negroes. The Amendment also stipulated that "the Congress shall have power to enforce, by appropriate legislation, the provisions of this article".

"The election of Ulysses S. Grant signaled the beginning of the end for both the Radical Republicans and the nation's interest in the fate of the slaves. The

---

[33] Debby Applegate. "The Most Famous Man in America", The Biography of Henry Ward Beecher". Page 357. Doubleday Books, Randon House, NY, NY.

Republican Party's original social activism was fast fading."[34] Within a decade, it would be the party of big business and laissez-faire policies. February 1869 marked the last great battle of the abolitionists, the passage of the 15th Amendment to the Constitution, stipulating that voting rights cannot be denied on the basis of race, color or previous condition of servitude.[35]

The Fifteenth Amendment to the U. S. Constitution was ratified on February 3, 1870 under the watch of President Grant. The Fifteenth Amendment stipulated that, "the rights of citizens to vote shall not be denied or abridged by the United States or by any State on account of race, color or previous condition of servitude." The Amendment further stipulated that, "The Congress shall have the power to enforce this article by appropriate legislation."

Passage of the Thirteenth, Fourteenth and Fifteenth Amendments should have ended all questions as to the rights of African-Americans and their place in history should now be comparable to other immigrants entering the United States, with one great advantage; that is, they were not strangers to our shores. By all that we have experienced, the first generation of immigrant children make great strides in achieving the American dream and by the second and third generations, all vestiges of the "old country" have disappeared and they have melted into the great American quilt.

Why wasn't this true for the American Negro? Because they were black! In all of human history, there have been slaves and slaveholders; however, in almost all cases, the slave and his master were look-alikes. Moses looked like Ramses.

In America's "peculiar institution," it was a black and white situation and that has never changed.

The American Civil War was won by the North and the Union was preserved and the Negro was emancipated; however the peace was won by the South. For the second time in American history, the issue of black and white was deferred to another generation of Americans.

---

[34] The Most Famous Man in America", ibid. page 383
[35] "The Most Famous Man in America", ibid. page 383

7

Redemption And Cruikshank

Redemption. A word and philosophy not commonly found in most of America's high school history books. Nicholas Lehmann writes, "The name implied a divine sanction for the retaking of the authority of the whites who had lost in the Civil War, and a heavenly quality to the reestablishment of white supremacy in the post-Reconstruction South."[36]

White southerners found redemption of their honor and pride by preserving white superiority in the south. By strategically nullifying the Fourteenth and Fifteenth amendments through the black code laws, or "Jim Crow Laws," and through violence, the southerners served the goals of the old Confederacy.

One of the great historical myths was that the Reconstruction Period after the Civil War was bad and that blacks were well treated and happy in the South. The myth was reinforced through congressional testimony by southern congressmen, by movies and novels in the early 20th century. *The Birth of a Nation* and novels, such as "The Leopard Spots," were specifically targeted to reverse America's impressions learned through reading "Uncle Tom's Cabin."

The myths of the evil of Reconstruction brought us the hero Jesse James, fighting for his family against Northern injustice. No film about Jesse James reveals how blacks felt about Reconstruction. The myth of Jesse James, "The Robin Hood of the South," is exactly that, a myth. Jesse James was, in my opinion, the forerunner to the likes of Timothy McVeigh, an American terrorist.

Missouri journalist, John Edwards Newman, romanticized and glorified Jesse James and the James Gang. John Newman Edwards, born in Front Royal, Virginia, became the adjutant for Confederate General Joseph Shelby during the Civil War, became

---

[36] "Nicholas Lehmann, *Redemption: The Last Battle of the Civil War* (New York, Farrar, Straus, and Giroux, 2006) page 185.

the founder of the *Kansas City Times*. Edwards was the single most important person to put Jesse James in the headlines and print in a positive fashion.

Edwards portrayed Jesse James and his family as aggrieved southerners who had been mistreated by Yankee "carpetbaggers" and robbed of their farm by Yankee railroad folk, who were supported by the federal army.

The real Jesse James, both during and after the Civil War, combined political violence with ordinary crime, targeting banks with ties to rival political groups, intimidating free blacks, terrorizing voters with reconstructive sympathies and, in general, trying to push the calendar back before the Emancipation Proclamation.

Over two-thirds of folks in Missouri were loyal to the Union during the Civil War, but the most aggressive Confederates, remnants of guerrilla leaders, "Bloody Bill" Anderson and William Quantrill changed the political landscape through bloodshed and intimidation. By the 1880s, Missouri, a border state with over two-thirds Unionists, became a part of the "New South."

During Reconstruction the Deep South was under occupation by federal forces and the state governments were dominated by the Radical Republicans. There were few, if any government troops in Missouri, Tennessee, and Kentucky, because those states had adequate native support loyal to the Union. The Radical Republicans pressed for the granting of political rights to the newly-freed black slaves. The Thirteenth Amendment banned slavery, the Fourteenth Amendment guaranteed the civil rights of former slaves and the Fifteenth Amendment prohibited the denial of the right to vote on racial grounds were all being enforced by Federal troops. Some blacks even attained positions of political power under these conditions.

White southerners thwarted black political activity and stood at odds with the ideals of the Radical Republican Reconstruction government. The early southern Democrats exercised their power through such organizations as the Ku Klux Klan and other paramilitary organizations such as the White League, or White Liners.

Somewhere in respectability between the White League and the Democratic Party were "taxpayer's leagues," which were springing up all through the South. Theoretically, the "Taxpayer Leagues" were merely concerned with what their members alleged to be excessive taxation levied by Republican authority. The "Taxpayer Leagues" were all white and appeared to coordinate with the White League.

The taxpayer's leagues always insisted that their goal was simply to put a stop to thieving by the Republican office holders, they opposed the main purpose to which the increased government spending favored by Republicans was directed: public education for the Negro population, which was meant to give the children of freed slaves the means to escape plantation peonage. [37]

After the end of the Civil War, blacks found themselves, "free at last!" America had passed the Thirteenth, Fourteenth and Fifteenth Amendments to the U.S. Constitution and they became free American citizens and were allowed to vote. Blacks flooded the polls, and in Mississippi's 1874 election helped the Republican Party carry a 30,000 vote majority in what had been, in pre-Civil War years, a Democrat stronghold.

The Democratic party of Mississippi developed a plan that was adopted by other southern states. It was commonly known as the Mississippi Plan. The purpose of the Mississippi Plan was to violently overthrow the Republican Party in order to redeem the State of Mississippi.

In 1875, the Mississippi Plan had two objectives, each quite simple:

1. Intimidate by fear any whites supporting or working with the Republican Party. Carpetbaggers were told to switch parties or switch States!

2. Intimidate the black population, who just recently began to vote and aspire to public office.

In regards to whites, applied economic pressure convinced most whites to transfer their allegiance to the Democrats.

In regards to blacks, Democrats were not interested in them joining their party, so a different tactic had to be used. They simply murdered blacks who dared to vote or get involved in civic causes.

Despite the 1874 Republican victory and the election of blacks to many offices including ten of thirty-six seats in the state legislature, the strategies of the Mississippi Plan had already been set in Vicksburg, Mississippi.

Vicksburg, the scene of great Civil War battles in 1862 and 1863 certainly felt the need for redemption. The White Man's party, with the use of rifles, prevented blacks from voting and successfully defeated all Republican city officials in August. By December, the Democrats forced the black sheriff to flee to the state capitol. Blacks who rallied to the city to aid the sheriff also had to flee against superior force. Over

---

[37] Nicholas Lehmann, *"Redemption: The Last Battle of the Civil War" (New York, Farrar, Straus, and Giroux, 2006) page 82-83.*

a few days, armed gangs murdered up to 300 blacks in the city's vicinity. The federal government sent a company of troops to the city in January to quell the violence and allow the sheriff's safe return.

There was never a white man tried or convicted of the crime of murder against a black man during this period, giving a clear message that the killing of blacks would not be followed with punishment.

There was no proportional action to the slaughter of 300 blacks in Mississippi, nor of the hundreds that were murdered in neighboring Louisiana in the infamous Colfax County incident. In fact, today, in the 21st century, there remains a memorial in Colfax which states:

Remembrance

**Erected
To the Memory of
The Heroes**

**Stephen Decatur Parish
James West Hadnot
Sidney Harris**

**Who fell in the Colfax
Riot fighting for
White Supremacy**

April 13, 1873

Let it be noted that in the "Battle of Colfax," over 200 blacks were killed, many of them after surrendering and unarmed, and three white men were killed. It is the three white men who are memorialized by the citizens of Colfax, Grants Parish, Louisiana. Interesting is that Colfax was named for the Vice President of the United States under President U.S. Grant, whose name is used for the Parish.[38]

In 1875, General Philip Sheridan, the great Union cavalryman of the Civil War, was sent to Louisiana by President Grant to try to restore order "he made a careful

---

[38] [Nicholas Lehmann, *Redemption: The Last Battle of the Civil War (New York, Farrar, Straus, and Giroux, 2006).*

America's Original Sin 57

investigation and reported that since the end of the war, 2,141 Negroes had been killed by whites in Louisiana and 2,115 wounded—all these crimes going unpunished."[39]

Although there was a call for federal troops to curb the violence, this time it went unanswered by President Grant, for fear that, in doing so, he would be accused of "bayonet rule"—which he believed would undoubtedly be exploited by Democrats to carry Ohio in that year's state elections. Ultimately, the violence went unchecked and the plan worked just as it had been intended: the Republican victory of 30,000 votes in 1874 was transformed into a Democrat majority of 30,000 by 1875. Folks had been given an offer they could not refuse.

In the spring of 1876, General George Armstrong Custer, a Union Civil War Hero, led his 7th Cavalry into the Black Hills of South Dakota. In the well known story of the times, 210 soldiers under Custer's command, including Custer, were "massacred" by the Indians. America called it "the worst American military defeat" of all time and demanded retribution. President U.S. Grant followed the American outrage by pulling troops from the "Reconstructed South," to invade the Indian lands of the Dakotas, and redrew boundaries that now allowed white settlement in heretofore Indian land. He literally permitted the slaughter of the native peoples of that area in retribution for "Custer's Last Stand."

The Presidential elections of 1876 were the most disputed in American history, more so than the Bush-Gore election of 2000. The election ended in a flat footed tie and had to be settled by a committee set up by the House of Representatives. Rutherford B. Hayes, Republican Governor from Ohio, needed the electoral votes from contested states of Louisiana, South Carolina and Florida. The Great Compromise of 1877, one hundred plus one years after the signing of the Declaration of Independence, was agreed upon by former Confederates (Democrats) and the Republican Party.

Rutherford B. Hayes agreed to pull all Federal troops out of the south and the southern states gave him the Presidency. The Reconstruction period was over in 1877 and the South, for all intents and purposes, nullified the Fourteenth and Fifteenth amendments with respect to our black citizens.

When Rutherford B. Hayes was sworn in as our nineteenth President, no violent resistance erupted in the South, as had happened 16 years earlier over the election of Abraham Lincoln. In return for the White House, Hayes agreed that the federal government would not interfere with southern whites and "their race problems."

---

[39] [Nicholas Lehmann, *Redemption: The Last Battle of the Civil War* (New York, Farrar, Straus, and Giroux, 2006).

Hayes wanted to leave the South alone because, unlike Grant, he had no interest in fostering interracial democracy. "Hayes opposed the idea of 'forcing' the races together, believing that the 'let alone policy' was the 'true course.' Hayes accepted southern leaders' rhetoric that they would maintain peace and abide by the law. He described his southern strategy as one of trust: "My policy is trust—peace, and to put aside the bayonet."[40] Apparently, bayonets were reserved to strike down railroad strikers in the north and against Native Americans in the west. [41]

There was no end in sight to the American dichotomy.

The agreement that the Republican Party made with southern politicians in 1877 completely turned them away from Lincoln's vision of *government of the people, by the people, and for the people, and his vision of a "New Birth of Freedom."* Abolitionists and reformers who led the fight to free the slaves were unprepared for the post-bellum situations concerning black and white issues.

Abraham Lincoln's military forces preserved the Union, however, Jefferson Davis' remnants reclaimed the South and returned it to the "good ol' days." Presidents Grant and Hayes followed appeasement policies that encouraged resistance to Reconstruction and weakened Republican resolve to protect the civil rights of the former slaves. Despite the presence of federal troops in southern states, the Ku Klux Klan and other groups that vowed to "redeem" the South were able to terrorize and murder blacks with virtual impunity. "The Supreme Court's decision in United States v. Cruikshank, handed down in 1876, simply underscored the fact that no branch of the federal government would offer southern blacks any protection from the reign of terror that would sweep the region."[42]

How could this happen? Are we not a nation of laws and not of men? The federal government had recently passed laws, the Enforcement Acts, designed to protect former slaves and allow them the right to assemble, bear arms and vote. The Fourteenth Amendment gave blacks the full protections of the Bill of Rights, including the right to bear arms, the right to peaceably assemble and gave them full due process rights.

Whites were arrested and indicted as a result of the Colfax incidents for depriving blacks of those rights and their cases eventually found their way to the U.S. Supreme

---

[40] The Age of Lincoln", et.al. page 311
[41] "The Age of Lincoln", et.al. page 311-312
[42] Peter Irons. "A PEOPLE'S HISTORY OF THE SUPREME COURT", Penguin Books, 375 Hudson Street, N.Y, N.Y.10014] Page 206,

Court. Cruickshank was one of the defendants indicted for depriving blacks of their civil rights.

Remember, murder was not a federal offense, so the folks who murdered blacks in Colfax, Louisiana were indicted for depriving black folk of the privileges of the First, Second and Fourteenth Amendment.

The Supreme Court decided that the Bill of Rights was not as clear as one might believe. They ruled on the side of Cruikshank and used the following logic:

A person was a citizen of the United States and a citizen of the state in which they resided. The First Amendment right to assembly "was not intended to limit the powers of the State governments in respect to their own citizens" and that the Second Amendment "has no other effect than to restrict the powers of the national government."

The Court ruled that the Constitution prevented the Federal government from depriving individuals from voting, or depriving individuals from lawful assembly or depriving individuals from bearing arms.

The Constitution, they ruled, did not address what individual citizens did to other individual citizens and the Federal government was not empowered to force individuals to act in a way determined by government. In other words, folks could do what they pleased and the government could not do anything about it, unless there was a State law, or local law that prohibited that activity.

This was the genesis of Black Code Laws and Jim Crow Laws. Local and state governments conspired to deprive blacks of all rights previously given to them by the Thirteenth, Fourteenth and Fifteenth Amendments to the U.S. Constitution as a result of the Cruikshank decision and have argued for the primacy of states rights ever since.

In the final analysis, blacks in the south were left to the mercy of increasingly hostile state governments. From 1890 to 1908, the "old Confederacy" passed laws to suppress black voting with provisions for poll taxes, residency requirements, literacy tests and grandfather clauses that effectively disfranchised blacks and, interestingly, poor whites.

Disfranchisement also meant that blacks could not serve on juries or hold political office, each of which were reserved to registered voters.

The impact of Cruickshank can be seen quite clearly in the 1936 Presidential election. Eighty percent of eligible women voted in the election of 1936 and one-percent of eligible blacks voted in the same election. Women became eligible to vote in 1920, blacks in 1870.

The Cruikshank case effectively enabled political parties' use of paramilitary forces. Jesse James and the Ku Klux Klan were now empowered to terrorize citizens without interference from the federal government.

8

A Cotton Curtain

To emulate Winston Churchill: *From Jamestown in the Old Dominion to the Panhandle in Texas a cotton curtain has descended across the Continent. Behind that line lie all the capitals of the old Confederacy, Austin, Little Rock, Jackson, Montgomery, Baton Rouge, Atlanta, Raleigh, Tallahassee, and Nashville. All these famous cities and the populations around them lie in what I must call the New South, and all are subject in one form or another, not only to the old confederate influence, but to a very high and, in some cases, increasing measure of indifference and apathy from Washington, D.C.*

In 1870, the population of the United States was thirty-nine million people, which included 4.8 million black folk, or 12.7 percent of the total population. In the former Confederacy, there was a total population of 12.3 million people, which included 4.4 million black citizens which constituted 36 percent of the total southern population.

Enough Republicans sided with the Democrats in Congress to prevent the use of federal power to assure African Americans meaningful liberty in the south. Imbued with widespread northern self-interest and apathy towards the problems of others, including racial prejudice, Congress gradually acceded to southern demands. It returned power in the South to white elites who claimed that they were better suited to handle their own institutions of state and local government.

Northerners, and society in general, were also quick to believe southern whites who told them tales of lazy, freed peoples. Southern legislators began weaving the myths about blacks that was accepted as fact by their brethren legislators; myths such as blacks were reluctant to work hard all day, and that they would take too many breaks and they lacked ambition. Blacks needed to be told what to do consistently as they lacked initiative. They needed to be nurtured and cared for, as they did not know how to take care of themselves.

Non-southerners also quickly believed southerners, who explained their reasoning about black folks, inasmuch, they claimed, as that they had lived among blacks all their lives. They knew blacks, understood them, and had no problem taking care of them.

White Southerners claimed that black politicians were more prone to be corrupt or at least, less able to prevent corruption, as blacks had little or no experience in politics. They blamed black neighborhoods for the violence against them, as blacks were asking for too much, too fast. They claimed that black suffrage was a failure as blacks did not understand the issues and could be too easily manipulated or their votes could be easily bought.

It was not much different than it is today; politicians of a certain ilk will uniformly repeat a reputed fact, and they repeat it long and loud often enough, that the general population accepts their version of the truth as fact.

Northern society was willing to accept southern truth as fact with respect to colored people.

What a difference a presidential election makes! In a single year, 1873, more than one thousand federal prosecutions were launched under the Federal Enforcement Acts, which ensured the rights of the Fourteenth Amendment were carried out, which reduced the effectiveness of the Ku Klux Klan. However, in the decade after the end of Reconstruction, the number of federal prosecutions averaged less than one hundred a year. The KKK was revitalized and emboldened.[43]

Was the federal government reluctant to carry out its own laws or was there another reason?

This venture into interracial, intercultural democracy was a failure to the delight of many in the south. Unfortunately, they were aided and abetted by the Supreme Court who placed its stamp of approval on the failure.

The Supreme Court ruled that the Fourteenth Amendment, which was designed to extend various legal and civil rights to former slaves, did not supersede the principle of federalism. In other words, the federal government could no longer discriminate against African Americans, but state governments were free to do so. Because most civil rights, including voting rights, fell under state citizenship, this decision allowed Southern states to continue to deprive black citizens of equal rights.

In 1876, the Supreme Court ruled that the Fifteenth Amendment, designed to grant male former slaves the right to vote, did not guarantee them the absolute right to

---

[43] "The Age of Lincoln", et. al. page 313

vote, but only the general right not to be discriminated against. This meant that the state governments were not obliged to protect black voters from the terrorist tactics of the Ku Klux Klan and other groups. This decision also played a significant role in bringing Southern Reconstruction to an end.

In 1883, the Supreme Court decreed that the 1875 Civil Rights Act, which prohibited racial discrimination in hotels and other public accommodations, was unconstitutional; in the Court's view, the Thirteenth and Fourteenth Amendments did not give Congress the power to outlaw discrimination in public accommodations.

Why did the party of Lincoln, the party of Abolitionists, the party of individual freedom abandon the African American to his former masters? Among other reasons, the main one might be basic Republican ideology. The weakness of Lincoln's new meaning of freedom was that it has to be vigorously defended. Republican free labor ideology, which had provided the political support for the eradication of slavery and the passage of laws granting black male civil rights, had never condoned government intervention to enforce workers' rights.

In Republican ideology, the federal government had no right to interfere in purely local issues; albeit, that local issues might be terror, mayhem or the disfranchisement of a total population was irrelevant *and probably exaggerated*. It was not until the era of television, in the 1950's when the American people were sickened with what was going on in the South did the Republican Party act affirmatively to preserve civil rights of black Americans.

Aware of the horrendous assault on black Americans rights in the South, and with no recourse in the federal judiciary for enforcement, Congressman Henry Cabot Lodge offered practical steps towards enforcement of the Fifteenth Amendment. The Massachusetts Republican, who scorned corruption of all kind—in business, in politicians and in elections—sponsored the 1890 Federal Election Bill to ensure fair state elections.

Republicans, in the House of Representatives, wanting to support their black American constituency in the south and wanting to protect their Republican majority passed the Cabot Bill by a narrow margin. But by one vote, the Senate failed to pass the Federal Election Bill, the last attempt by the party of Lincoln to protect black voting rights. Its defeat in Congress informed southern politicians that the reformers could no longer muster enough votes to advance black rights in the southern states. While many southerners wanted racial justice, justice could not be secured without use of the ballot. Power comes from the voting booth and a fair society comes only from fair elections. "The federal government had to be willing to ensure that African Americans procured an honest ballot. That it was unable and unwilling to do."[44]

In 1893, Congress repealed laws allowing federal supervisors to investigate voter fraud or federal soldiers to protect the right to vote. The next stage of white restoration was legal disfranchisement. White supremacy demanded that political power belong to whites alone, and southern whites preferred a racially constructed rule of law to an informal system of terror and fraud. Throughout the Deep South, white Democrats organized new constitutional conventions, this time to codify African American disfranchisement.

Remember "Government of the People, by the people and for the People?" The words of Abraham Lincoln were put to the test in the Deep South. When Mississippi's 1890 state convention passed a new constitution, delegates decided that statewide ratification was not required. Neither did South Carolina nor Louisiana require ratification. Southern leaders did not trust the majority of whites in their own states to do their bidding.

"In Louisiana, Governor Murphy Foster bragged to that State's legislature in 1898, "the White supremacy for which we have so long struggled . . . . is now crystallized into the constitution."[45]

By the end of the 1890's, African American disfranchisement in the Deep South was nearly complete. The South had risen again. White Democrats had succeeded to reclaim the South, in spite of the beautiful words of the Declaration of Independence; no longer would all men be created equal, endowed by their creator to certain inalienable rights, the right to own property, the right to life, the right to pursue happiness for themselves and their families. Individual liberties were no longer open to every citizen of the South.

During Reconstruction, blacks were able to secure political positions such as policemen, sheriffs, judges and many blacks saw the Post Office as an employer of choice. All that changed as soon as the white politicians began writing new employment law and specifically excluded black people from most good jobs. Certain jobs were restricted for whites only.

The former black sheriffs and postal clerks were fired, but offered janitorial jobs, and any job as a skilled artisan was prohibited to black people and the newly developed textile industries were whites only.

---

[44] . "The Age of Lincoln", et.al., page 315)
[45] . "The Age of Lincoln", et.al. page 316

Many times, in protest of their new lot in life, blacks would refuse to work in their limited jobs, and used their refusal as a bargaining tool in labor negotiations. Unfortunately, labor relations and unions were not yet a viable vehicle to advance workers rights and blacks were arrested as vagrants if they held no job.

The advent of the infamous chain gangs in American labor history had its genesis in America at this time.

The use of convict labor, almost always black men, was a perverted use of the Thirteenth Amendment of the U.S. Constitution. Section 1. of the amendment states: *"Neither slavery nor involuntary servitude, except as a punishment for crime whereof the party shall have been duly convicted, shall exist within the United States, or any place subject to their jurisdiction."*

An accurate portrayal of convict lease labor was portrayed in a film titled, "The Shawshank Redemption" wherein the warden of the prison benefits monetarily for the use of the labor on state road jobs. He is further enriched when a competitor for those same jobs bribes him, so he does not compete for the same work.

The warden accepts the bribe and tells his benefactor not to worry because they have plenty of work to do.

"In 1880, Tom Watson, a candidate for the Georgia legislature, attacked the convict lease system for exploitation—'Men of high standing and great influence, governors and United States Senators, were making fortunes out of it.'"[46]

By this time in our American history, there were two Americas—one southern and one everything else.

---

[46] "The Age of Lincoln", et.al. page 319

9

Louisiana And "People Of Color"

Louisiana is a good example of what *could have been* and the best example of failed opportunities to become a true "City on a Hill" country. As Jefferson and Franklin commented on the talents and achievements of Banneker and black students and and Lincoln admired Frederick Douglass, American officials were surprised upon entering Louisiana for the first time and witnessing a thriving state made up of multi-cultural/racial human beings.

Louisiana was settled by the French and Spanish and colonized by runaway revolutionaries from the island of St. Dominique, present day Haiti and the Dominican Republic. In 1803, during the ceremonies turning the French territory of Louisiana to the United States, soldiers of the United States marched into the city of New Orleans for the ceremonial lowering of the French Flag and the rising of the American Flag.

The American contingency were astounded that the French Army was represented by free black citizens of New Orleans. Blacks and Creoles, armed with muskets, were a frightening scene for the American contingent preparing to govern the new American territory.

Freed blacks, mulattos, Creoles, Cajuns, Indians and white people were living in New Orleans in relative harmony under the French and Spanish rule, and in competition with each other for business opportunities. Creoles were descendents of Europeans, Indians and Blacks and their primary language was French. Many Creoles were slave holders, and many were politicians, leaders of their communities, and skilled tradesmen. Almost all were Catholic.

Almost from the beginning of the American take-over of Louisiana, there were separations by race and color. Newly arrived whites were concerned about the power and influence that French speaking Creoles exhibited in the city of New Orleans.

Creoles were landowners, tradesmen, slave-holders, and were influential in the governance of the territory.

After the War of 1812, whites began to assert their influence throughout the South and in the new territories. They introduced legislation forbidding interracial marriage, segregating whites from blacks in schools and churches. They also forbid "people of color" to congregate in meetings. Whites had a fear that Creoles and other free blacks, who possessed guns and a working understanding of governance, would organize all blacks into a power base that could eventually rule Louisiana and become an example for the neighboring southern states.

Louisiana, prior to the Civil War, was unlike any other southern state. It had evolved as a multi-cultural, multi-racial society although it was distinctly divided. Whites were in the upper privileged class, while free people of color, especially Creoles, were just below whites and in the lower echelons, of course, were black slaves.

"Creoles were free to move about as they pleased, conduct commerce and trade, buy and sell property, serve in the militia and attend church services, the opera, theater and Free Masons meetings.

Free people of color, Creoles, were generally well to do, well educated, and dominated trades such as leather working, iron making, cigar rolling and carpentry. They also had their own journalists, writers, educators and orators. They owned significant holdings in real estate, invested heavily in banks and private schools."[47]

French Creoles, folks with French, black and Indian bloodlines, were already influential in the New World. The founder of Chicago, Jean Baptiste Du Sable, was a Creole, born to a French sailor and an African slave woman somewhere in the Caribbean in 1745. John James Audubon, ornithologist, naturalist and writer was born in Haiti in 1756, the natural son of a French slave trader and a Creole woman. Audubon's mother was killed in a slave insurrection in Haiti.

Edmund Dede was a musical prodigy; however, he had to leave America, because as a black man he had limited opportunities. In Europe, he became famous as a musician-composer.

Creoles in New Orleans read books by Alexandre Dumas, the author of *The Three Musketeers, The Count of Monte Cristo,* and *The Man in the Iron Mask.* Dumas's grandfather was a French nobleman and his grandmother was an Afro-Caribbean, who had been a black slave in the French colony of Santo Domingo, present day Haiti.

---

[47] Louisiana Cultural Vistas, winter 2001-2002, Mary Gehman,

Creoles in Louisiana considered themselves equal to whites, but accepted the separation of the *races,* as long as they were treated as free people and superior to the darker black freemen or slaves. Whites, however, fearing an alliance between free people of color and rebellious slaves asserted their authority, given to them by the Federal government and limited freedoms to all people of color. There was white and there was black. A black was any person *with one drop of black blood.*

The new incoming government in New Orleans brought new laws and a new culture; it required free people of color to register with local municipal officers so that their numbers, locations and professions could be monitored. Creoles were shocked to learn that it was illegal for them to assemble in groups and were not allowed to travel outside Louisiana without advanced notice to the state.

Creoles, especially the darker ones, had to carry paper proving they were free people and they could not conduct normal business and sign contracts, unless sponsored by a white man. And to further humiliate them, a 9:00 PM curfew was imposed on Creoles, the same as it had been on slaves.

Creoles, who were almost as equal as whites, now found themselves almost as unequal as slaves.

"Free people of color from Louisiana were outraged by these restrictions and many began liquidating their real estate and business holdings and transferring the proceeds to foreign banks. Free blacks with young families and long futures ahead of them saw greater opportunities beyond the borders of Louisiana and prepared to leave north, east, west and south to Mexico." [48]

What had happened to Creoles in Louisiana could have served as a blueprint for Nazi Germany in 1932 in regards to their Jewish citizens.

Louisiana became a state in 1813 and part of the Deep South. Ironically, it was General Pierre Gustave Toutant-Beauregard, a Louisiana Creole, who led the southern rebellion at Fort Sumter, South Carolina with the first shots directed at Union forces that began the American Civil War.

Francis E. Dumas, a Louisiana Creole, was the highest non-white ranking officer in the Civil War. Major Dumas was in the 1st Regiment of the Louisiana Native Guards, a unit made up of the colored people of Louisiana who fought with distinction with the Union army in the Civil War.

---

[48] Louisiana Cultural Vistas, winter 2001-2002, Mary Gehman,

A lieutenant, Morris W. Morris was also an officer and fought for three and half years with the Louisiana Native Guards on behalf of the Union Army in the American Civil War. Lieutenant Morris became an actor after the war and used the stage name of Lewis Morrison. He was the grandfather of famed American actresses Constance and Joan Bennett and the great grandfather of Morton Downey, Jr.

Louisiana's story is a tragic one. With so much culture, experience in governance, and harmonious coexistence, they could have been a leading example to other states of what was possible. Another great opportunity to "*Form a More Perfect Union*" was lost forever and the advancement of blacks and "people of color," with so much talent and promise, was stunted, and their growth retarded. Whites, fearful of loss of power, fearful of miscegenation, fearful of being the minority in a world where the majority was people of color, began nullifying the Fourteenth and Fifteenth Amendments to the U. S. Constitution in Louisiana and throughout the South.

10

The Fourteenth Amendment

The Thirteenth, Fourteenth and Fifteenth Amendments to the U.S. Constitution were adopted to reunify the Nation after the great Civil War. The Fourteenth Amendment had the most far reaching impact of the three as it promised all Americans the "privileges and immunities" of their citizenship, regardless of the state in which they lived. Moreover, it promised those citizens due process of law against any attempt to deny them life, liberty, or property and guaranteed, for the first time, the "equal protection of the laws."

These three Amendments, the "Freedom Amendments", finally brought the promise of the Declaration of Independence, that "all men are created equal" into the U.S. Constitution.

> *All persons born or naturalized in the United States, and subject to the jurisdiction thereof, are citizens of the United States and of the State wherein they reside. No State shall make or enforce any law which shall abridge the privileges and immunities of citizens of the United States; nor shall any State deprive any person of life, liberty, or property, without due process of law; nor deny to any person within its jurisdiction the equal protection of the laws. [The Fourteenth Amendment, Section I]*

Unfortunately, the Fourteenth Amendment was hijacked by corporate America when a Corporation was deemed a person in court cases in Louisiana in 1873 and in California in 1886. As in any law, if not enforced, it is almost no law at all. Remembering that there were 500 thousand armed rebels returning to the defeated South, the Congress which passed these amendments looked to the Federal Courts to protect the rights of the black freedmen.

The *Slaughterhouse Cases* in Louisiana, in 1873, was about the rights of property owners to monopolize the meat butchering business in New Orleans. It presented the Supreme Court with its first opportunity to interpret the Fourteenth Amendment. It responded with an exceedingly narrow construction. The case did not involve

Negroes at all, but white butchers who were excluded by a monopoly granted by the Louisiana legislature to a New Orleans slaughterhouse. The white butchers therefore claimed that the legislature had denied them property rights guaranteed by the Fourteenth Amendment.

The Court held that the excluded butchers were not denied the privileges and the immunities of citizens of the United States guaranteed by the Fourteenth Amendment. The Fourteenth Amendment *protected only Federal rights,* such as "travel upon the high seas, governmental protection in foreign countries, and the availability of the writ of habeas corpus. Most rights flowed from state citizenship including the property rights of the butchers, and were not protected by the Fourteenth Amendment. Thus, as a practical matter, the definition and protection of the rights of citizens was left to the states. The implications of the *Slaughterhouse Cases* for Negroes were ominous and were to be fully realized."[49] Corporations were now "*persons*" and duly protected by the same statutes as citizens.

"The Courts refused the role Congress had assigned it. In an 1883 opinion overturning the Civil Rights Act of 1875 banning racial discrimination in public accommodations, Justice Joseph P. Bradley voiced the Court's prevailing sentiment: "Blacks must cease to be the special favorite of the laws." The laws had a new favorite. "There is nothing which is lawful to be done," Stephen J. Field, one of the five justices appointed by Lincoln, wrote in a later opinion that reads like an lesson on public goodwill, "to feed and clothe our people, to beautify and adorn our dwellings, to relieve the sick, to help the needy, and to enrich and ennoble humanity, which is not to a great extent done through the instrumentalities of corporations." The new Constitution, as interpreted by the Court, applied to economic, not civil rights. The "person" whose "life, liberty, or property" the Fourteenth Amendment secured was not the former slave, now free, but the corporation." [50]

That the Supreme Court admitted corporations to the constitutional company of "persons" is well known, even if few recall the case. *Santa Clara County (California) v. Southern Pacific Railroad (1886).* Generations of state, federal, and Supreme Court opinions have cited *Santa Clara* as establishing that proposition, weaving it into the texture of constitutional law. Legal scholars have concurred. "The *Santa Clara* case held that a corporation was a person under the Fourteenth Amendment and thus was entitled to its protection." Through a series of rulings after the Fourteenth Amendment's adoption in 1868, the Court used it to protect contracts and

---

[49] "Racial Equality" Laughlin McDonald, ACLU Foundation, Inc. Skokie, Illinois
[50] Jack Beatty. "*Age of Betrayal, The Triumph of Money in America, 1865-1900*" Alfred A. Knopf. *New York, NY.*, page 110.

corporations, but withheld its guarantees from those whom the amendment was pointedly intended to help—former slaves, black Americans.[51]

Hugo Black, Associate Justice of the Supreme Court noted in 1938, "of the cases in this Court in which the Fourteenth Amendment was applied during the first fifty years after its adoption, less than one-half of one percent invoked it in protection of the Negro race, and more than fifty percent asked that its benefits be extended to corporations." [52]

Succinctly, the Negro American, who was the intended beneficiary of the Fourteenth Amendment, had neither representation nor a champion, after the end of the Civil War. The champions of freedom, the Abolitionists, the Radical Republicans, who governed the South between 1865 and 1877, were now interested in other matters.

Northerners, motivated into keeping the Negro out of the North and in the South, where "he would find happiness and prosper," passed ordinances making it uncomfortable for the newly freedman to migrate northward. The first ordinances and signs that proclaimed, "Black Man, do no let the Sun set on you in this City", were in northern cities, especially in Indiana, Iowa, and Illinois, the Land of Lincoln.

However, the pinnacle of the new interpretation of the Constitution was just on the horizon.

---

[51]   Jack Beatty. "Age of Betrayal, The Triumph of Money in America, 1865-1900." Alfred A. Knopf. New York, NY. page 110.

[52]   . Jack Beatty. Age of Betrayal, The Triumph of Money in America, 1865-1900." Alfred A. Knopf. New York, NY. page 135

11

Railroads and Mr. Plessy

Harold Wilson became my best and most loyal friend during the years we worked for the postal service, and as only best friends can do, discussing race was not an unspeakable, verboten subject; in fact, we had fun discussing race and ethnicity.

A conversation with him one afternoon became a catalyst for me to write this book. I promised him that after that conversation, I would write a book someday that would explain "what had happened to blacks in this country."

Our talk was about Tiger Woods and other athletes of mixed racial heritage. Harold said Tiger was black! Derek Jeter was black! Alex Rodriguez? "He didn't know but was probably black! Manny Ramirez was black!"

I said that each of those athletes could decide for themselves what they were. If Tiger wanted to be identified as a "cablinasian," which he personally labeled himself, so be it! I claimed that a person could be what he wanted to be . . . . period.

Harold claimed that there was an official rule that said "one drop of black blood, makes you black."

I got so mad at Harold that afternoon, that I shocked my son who had accompanied me to Harold's home. I scolded my friend, Harold, for accepting the white man's definition as fact.

Harold had bought in to the myth created by whites in order to subjugate blacks. Harold, bought lock, stock and barrel, what he had been sold; that is, "one drop of black blood, made you black."

Harold was born on May 21, 1938 in Memphis, Tennessee, the son of a brick mason, who made a good living in the Memphis area. Harold's grandfather was murdered by lynching as a result of a dispute over the ownership of a mule. No one was ever prosecuted for his murder.

Harold attended a segregated high school, Hamilton High, in Memphis, graduated with honors in 1956 and attended Tuskegee Institute in Alabama for one year. He also enrolled at Memphis State College in his home town, his first experience going to school with "white folk."

While at Memphis State, Harold worked for the U.S. Postal Service in Memphis as a letter carrier, a position blacks were traditionally allowed to do.

Where did Harold learn that "one drop of black blood" determined his race?

Let us regress. The Old South was dead. There was the South before Appomattox and the South after Appomattox, a sudden death that was coped with differently depending on what part of the South it was. After Reconstruction, Black Code laws began appearing in the New South, slowly interfering with the lives of freedmen, and after *Plessy v. Ferguson*, the New South emerged.

As the nation had two issues to answer, what to do with the rebel states and what to do with recent freedmen, each community of the South had one question: How could they restore their community as close as possible to what it was before the "War of Northern Aggression?" White southerners were conservatives, who wished for small government and no government interference in their daily lives. Although from 1865 through 1877, the Federal Government did supervise the South, after 1877, the South managed itself.

Segregation was not a word in the American lexicon until late in the 19th century as each community treated the new freedmen differently. Certainly during Reconstruction, blacks had some hope that their lot was changing. Blacks had some political positions of power including jobs such as county sheriffs, county clerks and registrars of elections, councilmen, state and federal representatives and judgeships. All of that changed after the Compromise of 1877, when Federal troops left, Radical Republicans began losing elections in the South.

Meanwhile railroads brought a growing industry to the South as new tracks were laid tying community to community. In the beginning, passenger cars were integrated. You paid the fare, you took the ride. First class passengers who paid the fare traveled first class, until white women began riding the railways. White women felt insulted, and feared the blacks who were riding alongside them in first class cabins.

Intimacy was not necessarily always sexual in nature; closeness was also a form of intimacy and blacks crowded close to white women were a little too intimate for the ruling class. Segregation as a formal proposition began with the railroad industry and community pressure to provide separate railroad cars for blacks and whites.

The "First Class Car" that was reserved for blacks was next to the engine where smoke would infiltrate the passenger cars and it was also closest to the regular coaches where men of rough repute, traveling from job to job, would travel. These men, mostly white, would transverse into the "Colored Only" car and harass the black women, even propositioning them for sexual favors, in the presence of black males, who were powerless to defend the honor of their women.

Blacks complained and filed lawsuits to persuade the railroads to accommodate them equally as whites, but were unsuccessful. The pattern of segregation which began with "separate but equal" railroad cars spilled over into other accommodations, including hotels, restaurants, parks and schools. Segregation became a pattern of life in the New South and was an acceptable way of coexisting, even to those former abolitionists in the North.

The political transformation complete, southern whites moved to limit the freedom of blacks in other ways. Segregation replaced slavery and race relations were redefined for almost the next century, and not only in the South. Enforcement of the new laws began almost immediately, and blacks fought back through the courts. Although, there was no reason to believe that the courts were friendly to their side.

To repeat what I have claimed earlier, if voting is not a strength of the community, there is no strength in the community.

Prior to the new segregation laws, Creoles were free to ride trains anywhere they wished, and they could travel in the "First Class Cabin" as long as they paid for the ticket. No longer! In 1890, New Orleans passed a law segregating trains, and Creoles fought back. They planted Homer Plessy on a train, paid for his First Class Ticket, and waited for the predetermined action by the white police.

Why Homer Plessy? Homer Plessy could pass as a white man. He was light skinned, light enough to buy a First Class ticket, light enough to get on the train and sit in the white section; however just black enough to get noticed by the conductor, who reported Homer to the police.

On June 9, 1892, the *New Orleans Daily Picayune* reported that a Negro named Plessy was arrested for violating the recent laws prohibiting colored folks from riding with white folk. Plessy's arrest went according to plan, and Plessy v. Ferguson worked its way through the court system, reaching the Supreme Court in 1896. In ruling against Plessy, the Supreme Court, while not using the exact words, instituted the infamous dictum of "separate but equal." *The Court found that segregation was legal as long as the separate facilities for blacks were not inferior to those for whites.* "The most common instance of this is connected with the establishment of separate schools for white and colored children, which has been held to be a valid exercise of the legislative power even by courts of States where the political rights of the colored race have been longest and most earnestly enforced." In refuting the argument that white privilege deprived Black Americans of due process, the Court stated that they are "not lawfully entitled to the reputation of being a white man."

The Court decision was almost unanimous as only one judge dissented from the majority opinion, Justice John Marshall Harlan. Harlan, from Lincoln's birth state of Kentucky, alone articulated Lincoln's vision of freedom: "Indeed, such legislation as that here in question is inconsistent not only with that equality of rights which pertains to citizenship, national and state, but with the personal liberty enjoyed by everyone within the United States." Harlan echoed Lincoln in claiming that the preservation of one's own liberty depended upon the willingness to grant others' liberty, but it was a crabbed echo because Harlan could not embrace this notion without caveat: "there is a race so different from our own that we do not permit those belonging to it to become citizens of the United States. Persons belonging to it are, with few exceptions, absolutely excluded from our country. I allude to the Chinese race." Harlan found it offensive that, while the Chinese were allowed to ride on white train cars, African Americans who "risked their lives for the preservation of the Union" and supposedly have "all the legal rights that belong to white citizens" could not.

However incomplete his understanding of Lincoln's new meaning of liberty, Harlan did not mistake its likely momentum. "The judgment this day rendered will, in time, prove to be quite as pernicious," the Justice predicted, "as the decision made by this tribunal in the Dred Scott Case." But whereas the Dred Scott decision had aroused an uproar, no political leader used the egregiousness of this ruling to mobilize opposition as a political issue.[53]

Plessy v. Ferguson formalized and made segregation legal in the United States and such was practiced and accepted throughout the country. It was as if the Declaration of Independence had no practical application among civilized Christian people. *All Men were created Equal,* but whites were more equal than others through divine

---

[53] 'The Age of Lincoln", et.al. pgs. 319-320

providence. My friend, Harold Wilson, lived and was educated in the south under the umbrella of *Plessy*.

Plessy would finally be vindicated more than half a century later in the landmark case, *Brown v. Board of Education*. In a twist that only history can write, the case would be heard by nine justices, including John Marshall Harlan, the grandson of John Marshall Harlan who wrote the dissenting opinion in the Plessy v. Ferguson case.

12

The Spanish American War

Two years after Plessy and thirty-three years after the end of the U.S. Civil War, the Spanish American War began in 1898. For the first time after the Civil War, America had a common enemy that enjoined our soldiers from the North and the South fighting together in Cuba against the Spanish. Pictures in the press showed northerners and southerners, blacks and whites fighting against a common foe, helping to ease the scars left from the American Civil War.

Among the first professional soldiers to fight in Cuba were the famed 10th Cavalry, the "Buffalo Soldiers" of the West. The black battalion fought in Cuba with distinction winning five Medals of Honor. A call to arms from Booker T. Washington, American black educator and founder of the Tuskegee Institute, promised to rally over 10,000 black citizens to fight in the Spanish American War. Many black men who had fought in the Civil War stayed in uniform and were in at least four "colored regiments" throughout the Reconstructed South and "out west" fighting Indians. They were eager to fight in Cuba as many saw Cuba as fellow "Colored People" fighting for their own freedom.

The Spanish-American War was a popular war for most of America and recruitment was not difficult. Volunteers from both north and south formed most of our combat soldiers into common "American Units." The distinction of Union and Confederate was forever abandoned. The "colored soldiers" were eager to show that they too belonged, and for the first time, they too fought alongside northern and southern whites.

The U.S. Army who fought in Cuba was led by General William Shafter, a former Union Army General and his second in command was General Joseph Wheeler, a former Confederate Army General.

General Leonard Wood led the 2nd Brigade, which included the 10th Cavalry Buffalo Soldiers, led by Lt. John J. Pershing and the 1st Voluntary Cavalry, the Rough Riders, led by Colonel Theodore Roosevelt.

The "Battle of San Juan Hill" was a misnomer. The fight heretofore called "San Juan Hill" was really a battle on two hills, separated by low ground called a saddle. The hills were Kettle Hill and San Juan Hill—the composite called San Juan Heights.

The major battle was on Kettle Hill and only the Buffalo Soldiers fought on both hills.

The first American soldier to reach the crest of Kettle Hill was Sgt. George Berry of the "Negro" 10th Cavalry. Sergeant Berry took his unit colors, along with the colors of the 3rd Cavalry to the top of Kettle Hill before the Rough Riders arrived. Lieutenant Pershing was with the Buffalo Soldiers when Col. Roosevelt reached the top of Kettle Hill.[54]

Pershing would later write . . . . *"the entire command moved forward as coolly as possible as though the buzzing of bullets was the humming of bees. White regiments, black regiments, regulars and Rough Riders, representing the young manhood of North and South, fought soldier to soldier, unmindful of race or color, unmindful of whether commanded by ex-Confederate or not, and mindful only of their common duty as Americans."*[55]

Politics, discrimination and the American paradigm of the need for role models and heroes prevented a true representation of the war. Publishers William Randolph Hearst and Joseph Pulitzer, legendary yellow journalists who were propagandists in favor of the Spanish American War, made a hero of the Rough Riders and Teddy Roosevelt.

Newspapers would not sell if the stories were about black heroism; therefore blacks were almost totally left out the media. A well known picture of the soldiers who captured Kettle Hill was taken showing Teddy Roosevelt with the Rough Riders in the center of the picture and the Buffalo Soldiers to his left and to his right soldiers from the 3rd U.S. Cavalry.

Newspapers of the day cropped the picture to depict only Teddy Roosevelt and the Rough Riders as the heroes of the capture of San Juan Hill.

After the Spanish-American War, John J. Pershing became an instructor at the U.S. Military Academy and was surreptitiously called "Nigger Jack" for his command of the black troops in Cuba. Smarter heads prevailed over time and the epithet was changed to "Black Jack," although the intent remained the same.

---

[54] Frank N. Schubert. "Buffalo Soldiers at San Juan Hill." Derived from a paper delivered at the 1998 Conference of Army Historians in Bethesda, Maryland. Retrieved 09/07/2010

[55] Cashin, Hershel V. *Under Fire with the 10th U.S. Cavalry*, Chicago: American Publishing House (1902), pp 207-208.

> "The war against the Spanish, which so many black Americans thought might be a turning point in race relations in this country, in fact accelerated the decline, the loss of civility, the increase in bloodshed, the white arrogance. The major effect of the war seems to have been to enlist the North as an even more active partner in the subjugation of black Americans. The war brought Southern and Northern whites into contact with one another. They discovered, much to their delight, that they had grown more alike than they had expected. The war also brought blacks and whites of all regions into contact. They discovered, much to the dismay of blacks, that they were ever further apart than they imagined."[56]

It was as if Lincoln's vision of "A new birth of Freedom" was never said. In every section of the country racial hierarchy was the order of the day, with blacks obviously holding down the lower depths of society. The new "truths" about African Americans began to take hold among whites: If African Americans did not vote, they could not serve on juries, were not entitled to good jobs, were excluded from main street schools and not allowed to live in good neighborhoods. After all, blacks were always happiest among their own kind.

If African Americans were not able to understand the white man's politics, and were naturally corrupt and of low morals, they could not participate in politics. They needed to be taken care of as they were like children. Blacks were now isolated from white society, and white society had no problem in the new landscape of the "separation of the races." Jim Crow became a complete legal institutionalization of discrimination. "The color line was nationally drawn as Jim Crow replaced slavery."[57]

"Throughout the North and West, and mostly in the Midwest, towns that had welcomed African Americans during the idealistic Civil War and Reconstruction years now turned them away. Moreover, whites often decided to instigate an exodus of their African American populations by orchestrating attacks on the black community or a highly publicized lynching. These "sundown towns," policies . . . proliferated after 1890."[58]

Lynching, and fear, kept the system in place. Newspapers praised mob actions against alleged black rapists, calling the white lynchers "exponents of a law that is older than governments, and more venerable than the constitution of states. Blacks could be lynched for anything imaginable, including looking the wrong way or accidentally touching the wrong person. Almost any seemingly benign incident could precipitate

---

[56] Edward L. Ayers, The Promise of the New South, Life After Reconstruction. Oxford University Press, New York, N.Y. Page 334.

[57] Orville Vernon Burton. "The Age of Lincoln." Page 321

[58] The Age of Lincoln, ibid., page 321

mob action. In South Carolina, Governor Ben Tillman proclaimed, "Governor as I am, I would lead a mob to lynch the Negro who ravishes a white woman."[59]

After Reconstruction, the Democratic Party was the dominant political party in the old Confederacy and they retained their power through violence, intimidation, Black Code laws and lynching. The Tuskegee Institute recorded lynching of 3,437 African-Americans, as well as 1,293 white victims during the period 1880 and 1951. White congressional Democrats formed such a powerful voting block that they consistently defeated any bills against lynching. The new constitutions in the South effectively disfranchised most blacks and, consequently, poor whites. Disfranchised citizens, because they were not allowed to vote, also could not serve on juries, so both groups were effectively shut out of the political process.

According to an article in TIME, April 2, 2002, "*There were lynchings in the Midwestern and Western States, mostly of Asians, Mexicans, Native Americans and even whites. But it was in the South that lynching evolved into a semiofficial institution of racial terror against blacks. All across the former Confederacy, blacks who were suspected of crimes against whites—or even "offenses" no greater than failing to step aside for a white man or protesting a lynching—were tortured, hanged and burned to death by the thousands. In a prefatory essay in "Without Sanctuary," historian Leon F. Litwack writes between 1882 and 1968, at least 4,742 African Americans were murdered that way.*"

White America made a sport out of lynching, to the degree that by the turn of the 20th Century, photographs of brutalized, dead bodies were sent in the mail, capturing the burning and hanging of corpses from trees. *The practice was so base, a writer for TIME noted that even the Nazis "did not stoop to selling souvenirs of Auschwitz, but lynching scenes became a burgeoning mini-department of the postcard industry. By 1908, the trade had grown so large, and the practice of sending postcards featuring the victims of mob murders was so repugnant, that the U.S. Postmaster General banned the cards from the mail."*[60]

In *Without Sanctuary*, a book of lynching postcards collected by James Allen, Pulitzer Prize winning historian Leon F. Litwack wrote:

> "*The photographs stretch our credulity, even numb our minds and senses to the full extent of the horror, but they must be examined if we are to understand how normal men and women could live with, participate in, and defend such atrocities, even reinterpret them so they would not see themselves or be perceived as less than civilized. The men and women who tortured, dismembered, and murdered in this fashion understood perfectly well what they were doing and thought of themselves as perfectly*

---

[59] The Age of Lincoln, ibid, pg. 321
[60] Richard Lacayo, "Blood At The Root", TIME, April 2, 2002]

normal human beings. Few had any ethical qualms about their actions. This was not the outburst of crazed men or uncontrolled barbarians but the triumph of a belief system that defined one people as less than human than another. For the men and women who comprised these mobs, as for those who remained silent and indifferent or who provided scholarly, or scientific explanations, this was the highest idealism in the service of their race. One has only to view the self-satisfied expressions on their faces as they posed beneath black people hanging from a rope or next to the charred remains of a Negro who had been burned to death. What is most disturbing about these scenes is the discovery that the perpetrators of the crimes were ordinary people, not so different from ourselves—merchants, farmers, laborers, machine operators, teachers, doctors, lawyers, policemen, students; they were family men and women, good churchgoing folk who came to believe black people in their place was nothing less than pest control, a way of combating an epidemic or virus that if not checked would be detrimental to the health and security of the community."

After the great American Civil War, African Americans tried everything within their means to become responsible citizens. They joined the Armed Services, they began voting and involving themselves in civic matters, built churches and schools for their community, but were stymied by their fellow citizens, and not helped much by their government.

A story that came after Hurricane Katrina in 2005 is illustrative of the mindset of many folks who do not understand the circumstances that have existed over time. Apparently, two ladies were discussing the devastation of homes in the areas that were below the water lines of Lake Pontchartrain, and commented that people were sure dumb to build below the water level and not on the high ground. The truth of the matter was that African Americans were restricted from building and living on the high ground and were limited to housing on the lower levels of the city.

Likewise, African Americans who had been historically denied entry in certain occupations have been disparaged for not having good jobs. Prevented from attending the best schools in their neighborhoods, folks wondered why they were not as "smart" as white folks. Not having access to good doctors or hospitals, we wondered why they died at an earlier age than the general population. Being among the last hired and first fired, we wonder why crime rates are higher among blacks than others.

The Black Code Laws and Jim Crow days existed from 1877 until well into the 1970s, a period of nearly one hundred years. What was it like to be a black youngster witnessing his father being subjugated by whites, and what did a black father teach his son on survival techniques while living under these conditions? What irreparable damage was caused by Jim Crow and how is that reflected in today's socio-economic condition of black Americans?

The effects of overt discrimination were taking its toll and the oppressed black Americans would find it difficult, if not impossible, to catch up, unless there was an affirmative, specific system that would help them accelerate.

13

Playing The Race Card

Many African societies divide humans into three categories: the living, the living-dead, and the dead. The living-dead are those that have recently departed and whose time on Earth is vividly remembered by the living. They are not wholly dead for they can still be imagined by the living who can tell real stories about them and can even paint them from memory. The dead are those who have been dead for several generations and no one living has first-hand knowledge of them.

When the last person to know an ancestor dies, that ancestor leaves the living-dead classification for the dead. As generalized ancestors, the dead are not forgotten, but revered. Many, such as George Washington or Clara Barton can be recalled by name. But they are not living-dead and that is a difference.[61]

My point in explaining the difference between the living, the living-dead and the dead is that mentioning their indiscretions emote great passions when we criticize living or recently departed presidents. As an example, if I were to dwell on the negative actions of Ronald Reagan, many readers would dive into their bunkers and begin firing back, without examining their reality. Or if I were to list the indiscretions of Bill Clinton, other readers would take it as a call to arms. This is because we lived those times and vividly remember these presidents.

Folks are just more comfortable dealing with the dead, than the most recent past. Stories about Woodrow Wilson, as an example, will not be as controversial or beg debate, as stories about John F. Kennedy or Gerald Ford. I am going to deal with our Government and the failings of administrations who not only failed to advance the causes of Black Americans, but in fact, overtly assisted in preventing them from advancing.

---

[61] "Lies My Teacher Told Me", James W. Loewen, Simon and Schuster, New York, NY page 259

I have no interest in denigrating American Presidents, as they, for the most part, were and are honorable men, did some good things and some not so good things. My intent is to show them with respect to their relationship with the black/white issue and the progress made, or not made, during their incumbency. Did the President do a good thing or a bad thing when confronted with a choice, with respect to the honor and dignity of black people? Did they utilize the "bully pulpit" positively or negatively? Did they divide us or unite us? How did they utilize the various arms of government? That is how I will portray the presidents of the late 19th Century and the 20th Century.

Every president has had opportunities to make a statement or take an action when confronted with circumstances concerning a black/white issue. Most recently, President Barack Obama took praise and criticism when he sided with Harvard Professor Henry Gates regarding the circumstances when Gates was arrested in his home by a white police officer. When asked by the press about the incident, the President sided with the black college professor and said that "Cambridge police officers acted stupidly." In the short period that President Obama has been in office, this was the first opportunity to take sides in a black/white confrontation.

Other Presidents also had opportunities, but in my opinion, only Abraham Lincoln, Harry Truman and Lyndon Johnson successfully used the bully pulpit to advance race relations in the United States. Most other presidents failed to do so and in some cases they exacerbated race relations.

One can only imagine if Presidents Eisenhower and Kennedy would have taken the hands of black children in their own and walked them personally through school doors, race relations in this country would have been advanced dozens of years. Both Presidents weighed political realities before taking action.

Most Presidents were more overt in their feelings towards blacks. Woodrow Wilson was a declared racist; Theodore Roosevelt invited Booker T. Washington to lunch in the White House and received so much criticism from southern politicians that he never again invited a black person to dine with him. So much for courage.

William McKinley, 1897-1901

Any biography of William McKinley, Republican President from Ohio, will write that he was the last veteran of the American Civil War to be elected President. He is famous for his positions on tariffs and the upholding of the gold standard, as well as fighting the Spanish American War and annexing Cuba, Puerto Rico and the Philippines. The biography would also end with his assassination in 1901 and the passing of the torch to his Vice President, Theodore Roosevelt. What most biographies of Mr. McKinley do not discuss in any detail was his position on Plessy v. Ferguson, if any, and his actions concerning the first race riot since Reconstruction in Wilmington, North Carolina in November, 1898.

> *"Just before the turn of the century, in November, 1898, Wilmington, North Carolina exploded in the first major race riot since Reconstruction. The Wilmington riot followed an impassioned election campaign in which intimidation and fraud brought in a white supremacist government. Plans were drawn up before the election to coerce the Black voters and workers, and to expel the editor of the cities black newspaper. Two days after the election, as whites began to execute their plan, the riot flamed. About thirty blacks were killed in the massacre and many left the city. The white mob suffered no casualties."*[62]

President McKinley was a war protégée of Rutherford B. Hayes, and like Hayes, he saw an advantage of not alienating the white south. McKinley did little or nothing to address the aggressive disfranchisement and exclusion of black Americans from political power.

Another example of good preaching and little action was McKinley's denouncing lynching in speeches, but doing nothing about it in practice. McKinley did nothing to prevent continued anti-black violence in the United States and, in fact, ignored the violence by taking no federal action.

Theodore Roosevelt, 1901-1909

I have already made some comments on Teddy Roosevelt and I shall not repeat those stories, but comment on other opportunities that TR had to impact the lives of black Americans. Interestingly enough, TR gets high marks from our historians with his progressive ideas about business, the environment and character. Theodore Roosevelt has to be one of America's great presidents and we are rightfully honored by his presence as one of four Presidents sculpted on Mount Rushmore.

Unfortunately, it was events that occurred during his administration that the modern Civil Rights movement was born. As is the case of so many great folks, who have been judged by their great deeds, their positions and deeds concerning race relations are irrelevant by American standards. It matters little if a president is a bigot or not.

In 1906, black soldiers were assigned military duties in Brownsville, Texas where citizens subjected them to intense racial discrimination. As a result of a confrontation

---

[62] Robert A. Gibson. "The Negro Holocaust: Lynching and Race Riots in the United States, 1880-1950," Yale-New Haven Teachers Institute

between a local white merchant and a black soldier, the city of Brownsville barred members of the 25th U.S. Regiment from setting foot in the city evermore.

On August 13, 1906, shots rang out on the streets of Brownsville killing a white bartender and wounding a white police officer. Immediately, the blame of the shootings was placed on the black soldiers of the 25th Regiment. The white commanders of the military post investigated the circumstances and told the city of Brownsville that all soldiers were accounted for on the night of August 13 and none of them were absent from the barracks.

When the locals of Brownsville began providing "evidence" in the form of spent cartridges from Army rifles that they claimed belonged to the 25th Regiment, local investigators began believing their claims.

When members of the 25th Regiment were questioned, none claimed to know anything of the shootings, although considerable pressure was applied to make them "confess." The soldiers of the 25th were not given any type of hearing, trial, or the opportunity to confront their accusers as guaranteed by the U.S. Constitution. As a result of their lack of "cooperation," all 167 soldiers were discharged with dishonorable status by executive order of President Theodore Roosevelt and banned from ever working in a military or civil service capacity. The men were never given a trial and were judged as a group and not as individuals. This will always be a stain on the presidency of Theodore Roosevelt.

In order to not lose any votes for his party, Roosevelt did not release his executive order for thirty-six hours, until after the polls for the national elections for Governors and Congress were closed.

There are some books that mention some of the members of the 25th regiment were comrades of Teddy Roosevelt on San Juan Hill. "*Sergeant Mingo Sanders, a veteran of the fight in Cuba, remembered dividing rations of hardtack and bacon with Colonel Roosevelt after the Battle of Las Guasimas.*"[63] *Many of these soldiers removed from military service by Teddy Roosevelt were veterans of over 20 years. Their earned retirement pay was forfeited.*

In 1972, as a result of public pressure, the U.S. Army conducted a new investigation and found that the accused members of the 25th regiment were innocent and victims of race discrimination, by the local community and the President of the United States, Theodore Roosevelt. The President's order of 1906 was reversed. Many in America called the case against the black soldiers of Brownsville, Americas' Dreyfus!

---

[63] Edmund Morris. *THEORDORE REX,* 2002 Modern Library Paperback Edition, Random House Inc., New York, NY. Page 467.

The Nixon administration overturned all the accused soldier's dishonorable discharges, but refused to grant back pay in pensions.

The south used various methods to disfranchise blacks, even using falsehoods and scare tactics in local, reputable newspapers. The riots in Atlanta, Georgia in 1906 were a result of these tactics. The Atlanta newspapers would sensationalize every rape of a white woman in Atlanta, as if rape had become an epidemic. The inference was that blacks were committing all the rapes; in addition, all crimes committed by blacks were front page news in the press.

White folks rioted! Whites invaded the black neighborhoods, totally ignored by the city police, and murdered blacks, looted their businesses and homes, and destroyed what was left behind. Some blacks resisted, but were either murdered or arrested.

Some blacks were arrested for carrying arms, a right guaranteed by the Second Amendment to the Constitution. The Right to Bear Arms apparently was a white privilege.

Springfield, Illinois, in 1908, the home of Abraham Lincoln and where the Great Man is buried, was the scene of another race riot triggered by accusations of rape of white women by black men. The riot lasted for three days and resulted in considerable destruction of black property and seven black lives. Two white men were also killed during the riot; however, the only person brought to trial was a 20 year old Russian Jewish vegetable peddler named Abraham Raymer. Raymer was convicted for stealing a saber from a guard.

The race riots of the early 1900s were not unlike the pogroms of Germany in 1932.

The race riots of Springfield, Illinois led to the creation of the National Association for the Advancement of Colored People, the NAACP.

In his time, the charismatic Teddy Roosevelt was one of the most admired and influential Americans and was often quoted and paraphrased. He was John Wayne before John Wayne. In my own hometown newspaper in progressive California, the following two editorials appeared almost exactly one year apart from each other.

To set the stage for the first editorial, Pancho Villa had invaded Columbus, New Mexico on March 9, 1916. In the invasion, the Villaistas killed 18 Americans while the Army stationed nearby, killed 70 Mexicans riding with Villa.

In an editorial, dated March 17, 1916, "The Date Palm" newspaper of Indio, California editorialized:

> WE TOLD YOU SO. Now that is a mean thing to say, but it is true. Long, long ago, how long we have forgotten, we said that the only way to have peace in Mexico and to retain our own self-respect was to send troops down there and make those bushwhackers and brigands behave themselves, hang the cut-throats and establish a white man's government with schools, churches, and amusements and to protect life and property, and give the poor simple-minded Mexican an opportunity to live in peace.
>
> We said the people of Mexico were not capable of self-government anymore than the Filipinos or Haitians are. In fact, there is no brown-eyed race of people on the face of the earth that is fit for self-government, and "you can't make a silk purse out of a sow's ear."
>
> .... We would suggest to General Pancho Villa a suitable rally cry, "On to Mexico". Just think, gentle reader, of the folly of treating as a civilized nation a people who are capable of so gross an outrage as that occurred by Mrs. Maud Hawk Wright. Suppose she had been your sister, or your wife. How do you think you would feel about it?
>
> In the writer's opinion that one incident warrants the use of as many armed the government has. We say now what we said three years ago . . . "On to Panama."

Almost exactly one year later, there was another editorial in *The Date Palm* because the United States found itself in another skirmish. The British passenger ship *Lusitania* had been sunk by German U-Boats in 1915 where 128 Americans died, along with the sinking of seven American merchant ships by the Germans and the publication of the Zimmerman papers, America declared war on Germany on April 6, 1917 and entered World War I.

The Zimmerman papers were documents that outlined the German plan encouraging Mexico to invade the United States. Germany believed that a Mexican invasion of our country would have neutralized America from entering World War I.

Mexico obviously did not invade the United States, although encouraged by the Germans; however, I found the following editorial in the same newspaper that described brown-eyed people as incapable of governing themselves and called for a takeover of Mexico and "On to Panama," stating their position on Germany and American involvement.

> APRIL 16, 1917. The American Eagle is aroused at last. Its defiant scream can be heard the length and breadth of the land. It will be heard around the world.

> *Ostensibly America is going into the war to protect our citizens, our commerce, and our rights at sea. In reality, America is going to war in behalf of humanity, in behalf of the down-trodden of every nation.*
>
> *The war is not between the French and the Germans or America and the Germans. It is between militarism and democracy, between the opposing systems of human liberty and military slavery.*
>
> *So far as the German people are concerned, our hearts are full of sympathy for them. We know them as the very best immigrants that come to our shores. They are among our very best citizens. It is with gratitude and pride that we recall the part played in our own civil war by Carl Schultz, Fritz Seigle and the German regiments.*
>
> *The trouble is that the German people have been under the rule of Prussian militarism for so many generations that they are not their own masters. They do not so much as do their own thinking. They are nothing more than cogs in an immense war machine. That war machine must be smashed if liberty is to survive. If it requires all the liberty-loving people on earth to smash it, then we must bear our share. Let us do it bravely, with malice toward none.*
>
> *In all history of the American Eagle, its defiant screams have always been in behalf of liberty. It has never been heard in a cry for conquest. May it always be so. May its sheltering wings protect the oppressed of all the world.*

The invasion of Pancho Villa into the United States was an act of an individual combatant and his followers, while the belligerence of the Germans was by a sovereign. Why the difference, in tone, of our local publisher with respect to the two incidents? One may rationalize that the editorials were opinions of a small town newspaper and did not reflect a national viewpoint, until one reviews other writings from influential people.

Woodrow Wilson was the President of the United States when Villa invaded Columbus, New Mexico and when the U.S. entered World War I, and I will discuss his views on race. However, among the most admired and influential men in America was Teddy Roosevelt, especially by Americans living in the Western United States.

TR was an outdoorsman, war hero, and a true rugged individual. What he said and wrote greatly influenced American thinking well before he became President of the United States. After the Spanish American War, TR became Governor of New York and Vice President of the United States under William McKinley.

During the years 1889-1896, TR wrote four volumes of books called, *"Winning of the West,"* which depicted his thinking of Manifest Destiny and Westward Expansion, especially in regards to the annihilation of Indians.

One of his famous quotes, taken from a speech he made in January, 1886, was, *"I don't go so far as to think that the only good Indians are dead Indians, but, I believe that nine out of every ten are, and I shouldn't like to inquire too closely into the case of the tenth."*

Teddy Roosevelt's books were popular and well read throughout the country, especially throughout the Western United States. His books stressed the struggle between "civilization" and "savagery" and the centrality of race struggle. His support of Nordicism, the belief in the superiority of the "Nordic" or "Teutonic" race, reflected his views on race, which were also representative of the views of a great segment of American society.

In an excerpt from his book, "Winning of the West," Theodore Roosevelt wrote:

> *"The most ultimately righteous of all wars is a war with savages . . . American and Indian, Boar and Zulu, Cossack and Tartar, New Zealander and Maori,—in each case the victor, horrible though many of his deeds are, has laid deep the foundations for the future greatness of a mighty people . . . It is of incalculable importance that America, Australia and Siberia should pass out of the hands of their red, black and yellow aboriginal owners, and become the heritage of the dominant world races.*
>
> *"The world would have halted had it not been for the Teutonic conquests in alien lands; but the victories of Moslem over Christian have always been proven a curse in the end. Nothing but sheer evil has come from the victories of Turk and Tartar."*

It is no wonder that the press in my hometown would feel free to express similar views. In fact, one of the major streets connecting my home town to others in the Coachella Valley is named Miles Avenue, named after famed Indian fighter, General Nelson A. Miles.

We can't leave Teddy Roosevelt without mentioning the good things that he contributed to race relations in our country, and one of the interesting things about him that make him one of our favorite Presidents. We have already discussed the incident in 1901 when TR invited Booker T. Washington, a noted black educator and President of the Tuskegee Institute, to lunch in the White House and to discuss issues. The meeting was widely reported in the press and caused uproar in the South.

Roosevelt's prestige among southern politicians was forever damaged and never regained in the South. Although Roosevelt was clearly a believer in Anglo-Saxon superiority, he did not waver in his belief that people of all races could give him good advice. Booker T. Washington and Teddy Roosevelt continued their relationship over the years, but never again met at the White House.

Roosevelt also openly supported a bill in the New York State Assembly which allowed desegregation of schools in New York, personally noting that his children had been educated with other races and there was nothing wrong with it.

Roosevelt appointed a black American, Dr. William D. Crum as the Collector of the Port of Charleston, and when he was criticized wrote, "*I do not intend to appoint any unfit man to office. So far as I legitimately can, I shall always endeavor to pay regard to the wishes and feelings of the people of each locality; but I cannot consent to take the position that the doorway of hope—the door of opportunity—is to be shut upon any man, no matter how worthy, purely upon the grounds of race or color. Such an attitude would, according to my contentions, be fundamentally wrong.*"

Roosevelt also defended the Postmaster of Indianola, Mississippi, Minnie D. Cox, a black American. Minnie D. Cox was threatened with mob violence and was forced to resign her position. Teddy Roosevelt took action by closing the post office, ignoring her resignation and continued to pay her what she was due as if nothing had happened.

Teddy Roosevelt was a good man, but unfortunately, his support of Nordicism and white supremacy was widely known and gave comfort to the many Americans who believed as he did.

Woodrow Wilson, 1913-1921

In any ranking of American presidents, Woodrow Wilson is certain to make the top 10 in popularity, admiration and respect. His championing of the League of Nations, leading a victory in WW I and his political positions, including leading the way towards women's suffrage, rank him among the best of U.S. Presidents. Both Europe and the United States conduct foreign policy today based on Wilsonian idealism.

But how did Woodrow Wilson deal with the issues concerning black Americans? In 1856, Woodrow Wilson was born in Virginia, four years before the beginning of the American Civil War. He became President in 1913, forty-eight years after the end of the Civil War. He proved to be a dismal failure with respect to race relations in America. While President of Princeton University, he forbid the enrollment of black students—Princeton did not enroll its first black student until 1940. As President of the United States, one of his first actions was to eliminate black employment opportunities in the federal government. Wilson allowed his cabinet officials to segregate offices of the federal government, including having separate restrooms and separate drinking fountains.

Segregation in the federal government continued through each succeeding President until officially ended by President Harry Truman in 1945. Although Wilson was openly criticized by black Americans, he was also criticized by southern racists for not going far enough in restricting black employment in the federal government. When confronted by black politicians complaining of segregation, Wilson responded, "segregation is not a humiliation but a benefit, and ought to be regarded by you gentlemen." In 1914, he told the New York Times, "if the colored people made a mistake in voting for me, they ought to correct it."

Woodrow Wilson's *History of the American People* explained the Ku Klux Klan of the late 1860s as the natural outgrowth of Reconstruction, a lawless reaction to a lawless period. Wilson noted that the Klan "began to attempt by intimidation what they were not allowed to attempt by ballot box or by any ordered course of public action."

Although it is not clear whether Wilson's harsh critique of the Reconstruction period was colored by his personal racist beliefs, it is clear that his critique provided much of the intellectual/historical justification for the racist policies of the 20th Century South.

Wilson's roommate at Johns Hopkins University was Thomas Dixon, the author of the novel, *The Clansman,* upon which the movie, *Birth of a Nation,* is based. Indeed, Wilson's words are repeatedly quoted in the movie, which is notable for its blatant racism.

Wilson's attitudes and actions towards black Americans is totally ignored when historians rank presidents and in America's high school textbooks nothing is written concerning the harm he did to black Americans as he was one of the most shameful of all U.S. leaders and disgraced the office he held.

14

Heroes And Warriors

My father told my brothers and I tales of heroes and warriors all our young lives. We had a portrait of World War II War hero General Douglas MacArthur on our hall wall. We heard the story of Uncle Albino who was killed in action in France during World War I; Uncle Ned who died as a Seabee during World War II; Uncle Ignacio who was the first to volunteer for the Army from our valley at the beginning of World War II. Our uncles' brother was the first to be killed from our valley in WW II and the local American Legion Post is named in his honor. My father's stories of Elfego Baca and the Lucero brothers of New Mexico were among my favorite stories of the "good guys," and Dad's telling of the "Message to Garcia" tale are still vivid in my mind.

I have recently wondered if my friend, Clay Tribble, had similar role models and was he told stories of wondrous deeds?

My home area was the Desert Training Center for General George Patton's Tank Corp preparing for the invasion of North Africa. I remember tanks and soldiers in our neighborhood as a young boy and how in awe I was of them. As an adult, doing research in old newspapers of the 1940s, I discovered that my hometown in Southern California had strict restrictions as to the recreation activities of black soldiers. They were allowed on certain days to come into town and go to the movies. They were restricted to seating in only certain parts of the theatre. They could go to certain bars and could not rent homes in town. Black soldiers were permitted to enter night clubs in "Mexican Town" in Indio and on weekends. The Army imported black girls from Los Angeles to entertain them.

In the annals of human history, no one is more glorified and idolized than the warrior; not philosophers, politicians or statesmen. From Alexander the Great to Douglas MacArthur; David who slew Goliath, or Audie Murphy and Spartacus to the 300 Spartans at Thermopylae, warriors and heroes are at the top of our human esteem.

Inversely, cowards have been at the bottom of human esteem. No one respects or trusts a coward or traitor.

Even opposition warriors have a special respect among their foes like Rommel, Robert E. Lee, John Mosby (The Gray Ghost), The Red Baron and Geronimo, because we honor bravery and principled sacrifice. We need heroic warriors even if we have to invent them in novels, film or comic books. Even Jesse James and Billy the Kid are American heroic legends, and *"the dirty little coward, who shot Mr. Howard, and laid Jesse James in his grave"* is one of history's dastardly anti-heroes.

We identify with warrior heroes and shun cowardice in fear that if we honor them, it might say a little of ourselves. The coward is the anti-hero and sometimes is needed to contrast with the hero.

John Wayne made the Frontier West safe for white pioneers to settle; he fought at Wake Island, Iwo Jima, Normandy and in Vietnam albeit all in make-believe movies and John Wayne died a great American hero. Joe Palooka was the virtual *"Heavyweight Champion of the World,"* a white "All American Boy" character who ruled the boxing ring, in comic books, at the same time that Joe Louis was the real Champ.

I liked John Wayne movies and enjoyed Joe Palooka comic books, but I never felt they were real, but many in our society see their exhibited traits as the manifestation of the best of our culture. As recently as the 2007 election period, Chris Matthews of MSNBC describes one of the Republican candidates as a "John Wayne" type of leader.

All of us know of the poem, *"The Charge of the Light Brigade"* where *"in the Valley of Death Rode the Six Hundred"* and the story of Teddy Roosevelt and the Rough Riders of San Juan Hill and we have historically treasured their heroism. Ultimately, San Juan Hill made Teddy Roosevelt President of the United States.

The truth is that Mr. Roosevelt's total combat experience consisted of one weeks' experience and one day of hard fighting. In an act of historical irony, half the members of the Rough Riders were left in Tampa, Florida, along with their horses, and never fought in Cuba. The volunteers who made the charge up "San Juan Hill" on foot were joined in the attack by the 10th (Negro) Cavalry. The 10th, the famed Buffalo Soldiers of American West fame, never received the fame for the charge up San Juan Hill that the Rough Riders did; however, their commander—Captain "Black Jack" Pershing was awarded the Silver Star.

The Charge of the Light Brigade and the Charge of San Juan Hill, along with Pickett's Charge at Gettysburg are surely acts of individual courage by heroes; however, they are no more courageous than the acts of the 54th Massachusetts at Fort Wagner, South Carolina during the Civil War. The main difference regarding history is that the 54th Massachusetts was made up of entirely black volunteers, and U.S. history does not treat their heroism quite the same.

Blacks have done themselves honor wearing America's military uniforms, in spite of incredible obstacles of institutional racism in the Military and in American society. Freedmen and slaves were early participants in the various conflicts that sporadically broke out between the English colonies and their Indian and European rivals in North America. Although there were early colonial and national laws to exclude blacks and Indians from military service, in times of danger or war, white leaders willingly drew upon these manpower resources.

In early America, African Americans served with distinction in such major conflicts as the French and Indian War, the American Revolution and the War of 1812. Blacks served alongside white soldiers, but all black units were also created. Free blacks were paid equally to white soldiers, while slaves needed their masters' permission to serve and many received emancipation at the end of the war.

Numerous Revolutionary fighters of varied ethnic backgrounds fought for the independence of these United States, so why has the reality of this complex mosaic of the American Revolution remained so long dominated by myths? Perhaps the view of Scots-Irish Charles Thompson offers an explanation. Thompson came to America a destitute orphan and became the protégé of Benjamin Franklin. He organized Philadelphia's radical "Sons of Liberty," and grew to become a wealthy merchant. "Yet despite serving as secretary of every Continental Congress from 1774 to 1789, he was excluded from the new federal government."[64]

Thompson declined to write a history of the Congresses he had served after repeated prompting by many of the Founders. One of the reasons they hoped he would write one was that Thompson had been gathering vast numbers of state documents and private papers from members for all those years, suggesting that he was going to use them to write a history of the United States.

But finally he wrote to Benjamin Rush, saying, *"No, I ought not. Let the world admire the supposed wisdom and valor of our great men. Perhaps they may adopt the qualities that have been ascribed to them, and thus good may be done. I shall not undeceive future generations."*[65]

---

[64] Willard Sterne Randall & Nancy Nahra. *Forgotten Americans,* page 79. Barnes & Noble, New York, NY

[65] Willard Sterne Randall & Nancy Nahra, *"Forgotten Americans" Barnes & Noble, New York, NY* Pgs. 78 79

Every ethnic group and nationality in Europe fought in the American Revolutionary War. "A history of the American Revolution should present a rich ethnic tapestry, not an all white, all WASP pantheon . . . The British Army was preponderantly made up of Irish, Scottish and German mercenaries, with more Germans than Englishmen fighting on the British side. What would today be called ethnic Americans took part in virtually every military engagement. Polish-American sailors in the crew of the *Bonhomme Richard,* commanded by Scottish born John Paul Jones fought gallantly. Twenty Hungarian Hussars came to America to fight under their Polish friend Casimer Pulaski. Greek knights journeyed to America and fought as volunteers under the French Marquis de Lafayette in Virginia."[66]

Black folk fought on both sides, with each side offering them liberty and freedom, if they survived the war. An estimated 7,000 blacks fought for the Continental Army under General Washington, while nearly double that number fought for the British. Fort Mercer, an important garrison in New Jersey, was manned by two companies of Rhode Island Continentals, black troops, three-fourths of them slaves and black freemen under the command of a tough former Quaker, Colonel Christopher Greene.

Let me tell you the story of the Battle of Red Bank and the many ethnic heroes of the war that won our independence from Great Britain.

The Battle of Red Bank commenced on October 11, 1775, when 4000 Hessians attacked Fort Mifflin, down the Delaware River from Fort Mercer. After bombarding Fort Mifflin, General Howe, the commander of the British forces sent 2000 Hessians downriver to attack Fort Mercer. Fort Mercer was prepared with excellent strategic bunkers, artillery and sharpshooters, basically laying a trap against the oncoming British.

The trap worked. The Battle of Fort Mercer left 500 German mercenaries dead, while the Americans lost only fourteen men. The Battle of Red Bank was historically significant in two ways—(1) the French now saw that the Americans were serious in their fight against the British and offered aid unconditionally, and (2) the British, licking their wounds did not attack General Washington at Valley Forge in the Winter of 1775.[67]

The hero of the Battle of Red Bank, and later a hero in developing the defenses around fortress West Point was Tadeusz Kosciuszko, a polish military engineer. For his contributions to the American Revolution, Kosciuszko was awarded a personal black

---

[66] Willard Sterne Randall & Nancy Nahra, *"Forgotten Americans"* Barnes & Noble, New York, NY

[67] Willard Sterne Randall & Nancy Nahra, *"Forgotten Americans"* Barnes & Noble, New York, NY pg. 76

slave. "Tadeusz Kosciuszko's last battle in the Revolutionary War was leading black American soldiers in the last battle of the war in Charleston, South Carolina."[68]

Despite the contributions of black soldiers during the Revolutionary War, legislation adopted by Congress in May of 1782 restricted enlistment in the militia to white male citizens. All of the state militia laws also reflected the same restrictions. Among the reasons cited by later scholars for this decision were white fears about slave rebellions, the misguided belief that black Americans neither could fight nor would fight, concern that black military service would cause unwanted social changes, and the notion that the arming of blacks indicated failure of white troops. This attitude of limiting or excluding blacks became part of our American heritage.

In 1798, the Federal government issued separate directives prohibiting the enlistment of blacks for use on warships of the newly established U.S. Navy or in the recently created U.S. Marine Corps. These decisions were in complete opposite of what was in practice during the Revolutionary War.

During the War of 1812, these restrictions were ignored as the needs of the Armed Forces for personnel were acute. In September of 1813, African Americans fought during the Battle of Lake Erie, a significant U.S. victory. Nearly 25 percent of Admiral Oliver H. Perry's men were black.

Almost 1000 blacks in New York City helped to fortify the Brooklyn Heights approach guarding the town from British attacks in 1814. In 1815, two battalions of 430 black soldiers fought with General Jackson at the Battle of New Orleans ending the War of 1812. Two months after the war ended, Congress passed legislation creating a postwar army of 10,000 men, but no blacks were recruited. On the 3rd of March 1815, the War Department wrote disparaging remarks about African Americans in official memoranda.

After 1815, the federal government and various states prohibited the enlistment of blacks or mulattos from serving in the Army, Marine Corps or state militias. The lack of a foreign enemy, racism, the removal of any Indian threat east of the Mississippi, and the growing concern, particularly in the South, about possible slave rebellions all combined to exclude blacks from military service in the four decades following the Civil War.

---

[68] Willard Sterne Randall & Nancy Nahra, *"Forgotten Americans"* Barnes & Noble, New York, NY Pgs. 78

However, the U.S. Navy continued to use black sailors and they were totally integrated in their systems throughout most of the 19th century. Things changed quickly when John C. Calhoun, South Carolina Senator introduced a bill, in 1839, prohibiting blacks from serving in the Navy, except as cooks or as menial laborers. The bill never passed Congress, but the Navy reacted by imposing a limit of blacks to 5 percent of the Navy's total personnel.

The opening shots of the American Civil War were fired at Fort Sumter, South Carolina, on April 12, 1861 once again raised the question on both sides of the conflict, about the feasibility and wisdom of using blacks in a combat role. From the beginning of the armed conflict, both sides used blacks for a variety of essential, but oftentimes menial support tasks. But neither side expected the war to last long enough to warrant the use of non-white combatants. What ultimately tipped the scales in favor of black participation was this first truly modern war's seemingly insatiable demand for manpower, along with President Lincoln's decision to transform the conflict from a fight to preserve the Union into a crusade to abolish slavery.

When the Civil War began, blacks were not recruited, and in fact, were disallowed to "bear arms" at any time. When the war did not progress as the Union would have wanted, additional manpower was needed quickly and by the end of 1862 black soldiers were recruited and fighting for the Union. U.S. Colored troops fought with distinction throughout the Civil War and were awarded fifteen Medals of Honor.

After the Confederate defeat and surrender at Appomattox Court House on April 9, 1865, many of the Union's all-black units began to muster out; however, several black units were assigned duty in the former rebel states during the Reconstruction Period.

There has been some recent attention about the glorious actions of the 54th Massachusetts in the battle at Fort Wagner, but not much about the black troops who were the first to enter Richmond, the Capital of the Confederacy, and who conquered the city of Charleston, South Carolina, and the slaughter of 275 black soldiers at Fort Pillow by Confederate soldiers under the command of General Nathan Bedford Forest. The black soldiers were under "a white flag of surrender."

Over 200,000 black soldiers fought in the American Civil War and were instrumental in keeping our country united and not divided.

After the Civil War, Nathan Bedford Forrest was one of the founders of the Ku Klux Klan. In recent years, there has been a concerted effort by some in the South to celebrate his life. The attempt to celebrate his life and the continuation of the use of the confederate flag is an affront to black Americans. It is in complete disregard of their mistreatment and a reminder of their prior human condition.

In the 20th century, there were heroic actions during World War I when the American Expeditionary Forces entered the War in 1917. Among the most decorated was the 369th Infantry, the Harlem Hellfighters, an all black regiment under the command of mostly white officers. The 369th were among the first to arrive in Europe and were "loaned" by "Black Jack" Pershing to the French Army. The 369th fought gallantly at Chateau-Thierry and Belleau Wood. They recorded more days in combat than any other American unit in the war. Included in their ranks were the first Americans awarded the French Croix de Guerre, equivalent to the American Medal of Honor.

During World War II, the Tuskegee Airmen honored themselves with their exploits that are now well established in American folklore, however belatedly. American Negroes have fought in all of America's conflicts and their heroism is not invented, although, until recently, unheralded by American history; in fact, there has been an effort by our society to subvert the information or at the very least to distort it to suit preconceived prejudices against blacks.

15

Roadblocks To Glory

Hispanics recently complained about the lack of representation of World War II Hispanic veterans in the great documentary, *The War*, by Ken Burns. Much of the media supported a neutral telling of the documentary; that is, they claimed that no one looked at color or race in a foxhole, an American was an American. It made no difference how you told the story, with or without Hispanics, the story is the same.

Well, it does make a difference. Reflecting on the tapestry of ethnicities and peoples that fought in the Revolutionary War, history does not always tell the whole story. Commonly told histories of war have purposely eliminated the contributions of black Americans. Although black Americans fought, with honor and glory, to liberate France during the First World War, an official order from the U.S. Army prohibited black soldiers from participating in the Bastille Day victory parade in Paris.

If race did not matter, why were there attempts to subvert the fact that black soldiers fought and died in the "War to end all Wars?"

One of our great heroes and an American icon is General George S. Patton, Jr., memorialized by the 1970 movie starring George C. Scott. But who was General Patton, and how does he fit in this story of race relations? I theorized earlier that we are who we were, and General Patton is a clear manifestation of my theory.

George S. Patton was born in San Gabriel, California, a suburb of Los Angeles; however, his heritage is southern. The Pattons were an affluent family of Scottish descent and Patton's father was a personal friend of John Singleton Mosby, "The Gray Ghost" and hero of the Confederate Army. "George Patton grew up hearing Mosby's stories of military glory from his father and from Mosby himself."[69]

---

[69] Carlo D'Este. PATTON, A GENIUS FOR WAR, HarperCollins Publishers, NY, NY. Pg. 40

Patton's great grandfather John M. Patton was a governor of Virginia. A great Uncle, Waller Patton, perished of wounds received in Pickett's Charge during the battle of Gettysburg. Another relative, Hugh Weedon Mercer, was a Confederate General.

Patton's grandfather was Colonel George Smith Patton, born in Fredericksburg, Virginia, graduated from Virginia Military Institute (VMI), Class of 1852 and served in the 22nd Virginia Infantry of the Confederate States of America.

Dying at the Battle of Opequon Creek, Patton's grandfather left behind a son, born in Charleston, Virginia named George Smith Patton, the father of the future World War II General. George Smith Patton graduated from VMI in 1877, and ultimately served as a Los Angeles County District Attorney and the first City Attorney for the city of Pasadena, California and the first mayor of San Marino, California. The future General's father was an admirer of Woodrow Wilson and carried a similar nostalgia for the Ol' South and was disgusted by how Reconstruction had changed it.

It was commonly acknowledged that Patton Sr. publicly advocated the continued supremacy of the Aryan civilization, and no wonder, that his son, future General George S. Patton Jr. developed the attitude that he did.

"The Patton home in Pasadena kept paintings of Robert E. Lee and Stonewall Jackson in their home. Young George Patton admired them as he knelt to say his prayers, initially believing that they were portraits of God and Jesus."[70]

Patton's upbringing and conversations he obviously heard and participated in while growing up assisted in the development of his attitudes towards black Americans. The use of black troops during the rush to the Siegfried Line offers some insight into Patton's racial attitude. The 761st Tank Battalion (colored), commanded by Lieutenant Colonel P.T. Bates, reported to the Army on the twenty-eighth of October, 1944, and assigned to Patton. "As the 761st was about to enter combat, Patton reviewed the battalion and addressed the men:"[71]

"Men, you're the first Negro tankers to ever fight in the American Army. I would never have asked for you if you weren't good. I have nothing but the best in my Army. I don't care what color you are as long as you go up there and kill those Kraut sons of bitches. Everyone has their eyes on you and is expecting great things from you. Don't let them down and damn you, don't let me down."[72]

---

[70] Carlo D'Este. PATTON, A GENIUS FOR WAR, HarperCollins Publishers, NY, NY. Pg. 40

[71] General George S. Patton, Jr., WAR as I knew it. Houghton Mifflin Co. Boston-New York. Page 158-159

[72] George S. Patton, The 761st "Black Panther" Tank Battalion in World War II." Jefferson, NC: McFarland & Company, 1999, p 53)

However, like many men of influence over the years, Patton expressed his doubts about using black men in combat. On returning to Headquarters, he remarked, "They gave a good first impression, but I have no faith in the inherent fighting ability of the race."

Patton wrote in his diaries, which were compiled after his death, and released as his book, *WAR As I Knew It*, where he relates the interaction described above, and comments, "Individually they were good soldiers, but I expressed my belief at the time, and have never found the necessity of changing it, that a colored soldier cannot think fast enough to fight in armor."[73]

In later years, Al Campanis, General Manager of the Los Angeles Dodgers, made a similar comment on *Nightline*. When asked by the narrator why there were so few blacks managing baseball teams, Campanis stated, "blacks may not have some of the necessities to be . . . a field manager . . . or perhaps a general manager." Later in the interview, Campanis said it was his belief that blacks are poor swimmers "because they don't have the buoyancy."[74]

Perceptions are realities and those perceptions, unchallenged, have been the reality of heavy weight, influential decision makers in the United States for many years.

Carlo D'Este in his book, *Patton: A Genius for War* explains that "George S. Patton's writing can be read as disdaining blacks and their officers because they were not part of his social order . . . Historian Hugh Cole points out that Patton was the first American military leader to integrate the rifle companies 'when manpower got tight.' Patton's views on blacks seem mild and even generous compared to remarks he made about Jews and other ethnic groups he encountered throughout his military career. He generally considered those who were not of Northern European ancestry to be dirty and uncivilized."[75]

Never mind that Patton, during his many battles, was witness to heroic accomplishments by the 761st Tank Battalion, and the "Red Ball Express," who supplied him with fuel during his charge across Europe. Since an Army without gas, bullets and food would quickly be defeated, the Army Transportation Corps created a huge trucking operation called the "Red Ball Express" on August 21, 1944. The trucks started rolling on August 25, 1944 and continued with no let up for eighty-two straight days.

---

[73] Patton, George S. "War As I Knew It". Boston: Houghton Mifflin, 1947, p 160
[74] Nightline interview by Ted Koppel, April 6, 1987.
[75] Carlo D'Este. PATTON, A GENIUS FOR WAR, HarperCollins Publishers, NY, NY. Pg. 656

"Nearly 75 percent of all Red Ball Express drivers were African Americans. That's because well before and during the war, U.S. commanders in general believed African Americans had no mettle or guts for combat. Consequently, the Army relegated blacks primarily to safe service and supply outfits and the Navy assigned them as mess stewards. The Marines were combat troops and the Corps refused to take blacks at all until 1942."[76]

In 1952, Hollywood made a movie about the "Red Ball Express," starring Jeff Chandler and Alex Nicol, with Hugh O'Brien and Sydney Poitier taking minor roles. The principle roles were by white men with blacks only in minimal scenes. But like the argument being made about the documentary, *The War*, by Ken Burns, it matters who you see on the screen. It establishes attitudes and perceptions. Perceptions become people's reality.

The 761st Tank Battalion fought gallantly, the Red Ball Express drove valiantly, the "Tuskegee Airmen" flew courageously and successfully in support of our war effort and historically there is empirical evidence that blacks fight as well as any other group, and have the necessary "guts" and "smarts" to fight in the Air, Land and Sea. So why do educated people like George S. Patton, seeing the empirical evidence, say otherwise? Why? Because one's beliefs are one's reality, never mind empirical information and to say otherwise might be an affront to one's ancestors.

General George S. Patton slapped a soldier in France and was reprimanded. He insulted the Russians in a speech in England and was reprimanded. He "slapped" the entire black race from America and was not reprimanded. Unfortunately, his remarks about American blacks represented the American paradigm.

"That Patton expressed anti-Semitic and anti-black values is beyond question; that he was a racist is less certain . . . . he was a product of his times and clearly distrusted both blacks and Jews; the former were simply considered inferior, whereas Jews were distrusted and often despised for their success."[77]

The same could be said of many influential men, that they were not racists or bigots, but just "products of their times," and that would suffice for most. Unfortunately, the only folks injured by such comments, wherein beliefs became the fathers of the act, were blacks and Jews. We sometimes get confused—racism does not always stem from hatred; ignorance is also a fertile ground.

---

[76] Rudi Williams, American Forces Press Service, NEWS ARTICLES, February 15, 2002)

[77] Carlo D'Este. PATTON, A GENIUS FOR WAR, HarperCollins Publishers, NY, NY. Pg. 172

16

Integration of the Armed Forces

They were members of the same "Greatest Generation"—one a black man, John Hope Franklin, and the other a white man, Robert Byrd. When the United States entered the Second World War, John Franklin was 26 years old and Robert Byrd was 24. Franklin, who had just earned his doctorate in history from Harvard University, was starting to teach in Raleigh, North Carolina at St. Augustine's College, a historically black institution. Byrd, who would become the senior U.S. Senator from West Virginia, was beginning to work as a welder building ships in a construction yard in Baltimore, Maryland.

Neither one ever served in the military. John Franklin sought to enlist. Nearly a half century after Pearl Harbor, at the close of a distinguished career that culminated at the University of Chicago and Duke University, he recalled his efforts to join up:

> *"How best to serve became a question uppermost in my mind. The question appeared to be answered by the United States Navy, which ran a full-page advertisement in the local newspaper. There was a shortage of personnel to handle the crush of paperwork, the navy stated; and men who could type, take shorthand, operate simple business machines, and perform other office chores could look forward to early promotion. I rushed down to the recruitment office and volunteered to relieve the navy of its distress."*

The offer was not accepted. "*the recruiter looked at me with what appeared to be a combination of incredulity and distress . . . he simply said I was lacking in one qualification and that was color.*" After further nasty experiences, including the refusal of a doctor at a Tulsa induction center to draw his blood, Franklin successfully avoided the draft for the remainder of the war, having concluded that "*the United States, however much it was devoted to protecting the freedoms and rights of Europeans, had no respect for me, no interest in my well-being, and not even a desire to utilize my services.*"

Robert Byrd, who was born in North Carolina, and who, two years later, would be elected to the West Virginia House of Delegates, wrote a letter of concern about black demands for racial integration in the military to Theodore Bilbo of Mississippi, the Senate's most outspoken racist, in December, 1944. *"I am a typical American, a southerner, and 27 years of age,"* Byrd noted,

> *"And never in the world will I be convinced that race mixing in any field is good. All the social 'do-gooders,' the philanthropic 'greats' of this day, the reds and pinks . . . the disciples of Eleanor . . . can never alter my convictions on this question. I am loyal to my country and know but reverence to her flag, BUT I shall never submit to fight beneath that banner with a negro by my side. Rather, I should die a thousand times, and see this old glory trampled in the dirt never to rise again, than to see this beloved land of ours become degraded by race mongrels, a throwback to the blackest specimen from the wilds."*[78]

"Within four years, Byrd's nightmare had become a national policy. On July 26, 1948, President Harry Truman signed Executive Order 9981. Writing as Commander in Chief, he declared, the policy of the President that there shall be equality of treatment and opportunity for all persons in the armed forces without regard to race, color, religion and national origin." By the time the Korean War had ended, all the branches of the armed forces were integrated by race, though some all-black infantry regiments remained. By 1956, integration was complete. Today, the military is our country's most successful institution, least marked by racial separation.[79]

Morris J. MacGregor, Jr.'s book, *Integration of the Armed Forces, 1940-1965* is a history of the black experience in the military. A historian with the U.S. Army Center of Military History (CMH), MacGregor received his Bachelor's and Master's in history from the Catholic University of America. He also studied at John Hopkins University and the University of Paris on a Fulbright grant. MacGregor served for ten years in the Historical Division of the Joint Chiefs of Staff before joining the CMH staff in 1968.

In his book, MacGregor outlines the condition of blacks in the U.S. military. He draws upon four sources, including the Gillen Board Report, the Fahy Report, the Chamberlin Report, and Project CLEAR, to support his history. MacGregor states,

> *"This book describes the fall of the legal, administrative, and social barriers to the black Americans full participation in the military service of his country. It follows*

---

[78] Ira Katzenelson. "When Affirmative Action was White." W.W. Norton & Co. New York, NY. pages 81-82.

[79] Ira Katzenelson. "When Affirmative Action was White. An Untold History of Racial Inequality in Twentieth Century America." W.W. Norton and Company, NY, NY)

the changing status of the black serviceman from the eve of World War II, when he was excluded from many military activities and rigidly segregated in the rest, to that period a quarter of a century later when the Department of Defense extended its protection of his rights and privileges even to the civilian population."

The reader is reminded that there were segregated black troops during the U.S. Civil War, segregated black troops who fought with Roosevelt on San Juan Hill, segregated black troops who fought during World War I and segregated black troops who fought during World War II.

In October of 1945, the United States ordered the U.S. Army to review its racial policies. General George Marshall established a board led by Lt. General Alvan C. Gillem, Jr., to study the situation and prepare a directive on the use of African Americans in the postwar Army.

The Gillem Board, upon completion of its study, did not recommend that the Army integrate its' forces, because doing so "would have been a radical step, out of keeping with the climate of opinion in the country and in the Army itself." However, the Gillem Board established the principle that African Americans had a constitutional right to fight and the Army mission was to get the best out of each soldier.

In 1946, the U.S. Navy made black sailors "eligible for all types of assignments in all ratings in all activities and on all ships of Naval Service." The Navy also directed that housing and other facilities on bases, including the Mess Hall be integrated. A giant step forward in policy; however, African Americans continued to monopolize duties in the Steward's Branch and received no specialized assignments.

The U.S. Marine Corps is part of the Navy, but ignored the U.S. Navy directive and developed their own policies of continued segregation and racial tokenism. It would have been their greater desire to entirely eliminate African Americans from the Corps; however, not being able to do that the Marine Corps adhered to its tradition by limiting blacks to "small self-contained units performing traditional laboring tasks."

The "whites only" tag was relatively liberal as the U.S. Marine Corps welcomed the enlistment of many Mexican Americans during World War II. It is to the Corps disgrace that not a single Mexican American was ever recommended for the Medal of Honor during their service in the war, even though they earned the greatest number of Medals of Honor than any other identifiable ethnic group in the U.S. Army during the same war.

Not being able to ignore the Navy order to integrate the Corps, and its stubbornness to remain the same as it has always been, the Marine Corps established a quota of no more than 1500 blacks at any one time in the entire Marine Corps, and they assigned these black folks to menial jobs, especially locating them in the non-white Steward's Branch.

The Marine Corps did not change its practices until bullets began flying in the Korean War in 1950.

After World War II, the Army Air Corps was granted separate branch status and became the darling of the Armed Services. Remember, this is the service where the Tuskegee Airmen had so honorably served and showed their abilities. However, becoming the elite organization they had sought to become, it asked for a special exemption to exclude African Americans from its branch.

The Air Force did not get its wishes, but they did get a significantly lower quota of black soldiers, along with restrictions on the areas where they could be used. Quotas were a popular method of restricting blacks in all the armed services; therefore, once again eliminating their long term ability to benefit from the G.I. Bill that would have provided them an education and better housing.

It was peace time in America and in 1946, the Secretary of War suspended black enlistments in the Regular Army and began reducing the number of personnel in the Army. Using recently established criteria, it began eliminating the least qualified men from the Army. Guess who these were?

MacGregor noted that the U.S. Army, an agency of the U.S. Government, began accepting qualified African American recruits; however, the Army established a score of 100 on the Army General Classification Test (AGCT) for all African American enlistees, as opposed to 70 for whites. The U.S. Army used this method to limit the number of African American soldiers.

By 1948, The U.S. Navy's main racial problem was a serious lack of black sailors as they were unable to attract many African Americans in the postwar period. Blacks were now welcomed in the Navy, but they were no longer interested. Serving in the non-white Steward's Branch attracted very few black recruits.

In 1947, Army leaders in the United States began accelerating efforts to discharge soldiers who had scored less than 70 on the AGCT, supposedly in an attempt to close the educational/training gap between black and white servicemen. At the same time, however, Lieutenant General Clarence R. Huebner initiated a major project to educate and train thousands of African American soldiers in Europe. Did this program work?

It worked so well that white soldiers filed complaints of discrimination as they were excluded from these programs. This might have been the earliest charges of "reverse discrimination" in our history. The program produced some of the finest trained black troops in the Army.

In addition to producing better soldiers, the program had collateral success as the improved morale manifested by the black soldiers led to a decline in racial disputes, crime and venereal disease rates among black soldiers. Despite overwhelming success and the nexus between education and performance, the U.S. Army did not expand the program in any other area of their command.

Less than a year after the publication of the Gillem Board Report, Army leaders still considered segregation to be a policy worth retaining indefinitely. From their viewpoint, integration would only become feasible once the Army "completed the long, complex task of raising the quality and lowering the quantity of black soldiers."

Overall, the Army reported that it was providing access to schools and training to all its force equally. The truth was that most specialized schools were closed to black soldiers, irrespective of their qualifications. Numerically, the number of training spaces for blacks had declined, contrary with what the Army was reporting.

Senator Richard Russell of Georgia was one of many southern Senators who served as chairs in important Senate committees. Russell, an avowed white supremacist, served in the U.S. Senate from 1932 until his death in 1971. He along with Senators Strom Thurmond and James Eastland formed a southern bloc that stalled most civil rights legislation during their time in the Senate and did everything within their means to interrupt integration in the armed forces.

Senator Russell, who chaired the important Armed Services committee and the Senate Appropriations committee, introduced an amendment to the Selective Service Bill that would have guaranteed segregation *voluntarily*. His amendment would have allowed for white recruits the option to serve only with members of their own race.

The amendment was not signed into law, but served to show the intent of some members of Congress. The Selective Service bill was signed into law by President Harry Truman and the various Services began squabbling about the increased number of blacks that would come into their organizations.

In July 1948, the Democratic National Convention nominated Harry Truman for president, despite growing southern opposition to the strong civil rights platform accepted by Truman. Southern democrats bolted the Democrat Party and formed a third party, and called themselves, "Dixiecrats." They became a States Rights party, without a civil rights plank in their platform, and nominated Senator Strom Thurmond, of South Carolina for president.

On the 26th of July, 1948, President Truman signed Executive Order 9981, providing for equal treatment and opportunity for African American servicemen; however, the order had little immediate effect on the armed forces. Neither the Army nor the Navy planned to alter their existing racial policies. Their decisions were partly based on the mistaken assumption that they were already in compliance. Despite evidence to the contrary, the U.S. Armed Forces did not consider segregation to be discriminatory. The fact that Truman was not favored for reelection also influenced the initially low-key reaction to Executive Order 9981. Even Congress responded with a "wait and see" attitude.

In September of 1948, Secretary of Defense Forrestal decided that "inter-service integration was not workable." The reason it was not workable was not because of valid data observed in integrated units, but because top brass of the Army, Navy and Air Force strenuously objected to the concept of integration on the basis of efficiency.

The Navy rationalized their poor track record in attracting black recruits by claiming that "Negroes favored the Army because they were not a seafaring people." This claim blatantly ignored the Navy's own history, and greatly minimized the Navy's unwillingness to provide greater opportunities for African Americans or to integrate the Steward's Branch.

The racial policies of the Armed Forces were under continuing attack by black leaders and civil rights groups as the Army continued to rely on racial quotas. The Army argued that quotas on black enlistees guaranteed black participation in the service. However, the quota system actually limited the number of black Americans admitted into the service as well as the variety of training and jobs available to them. Conservative Army traditionalists seeking to maintain a segregated Army could not prevent all racial progress, but the use of quotas and the remaining restrictions on how black soldiers were employed made reform efforts very slow.

Despite a lot of "foot-dragging," the Army confronted and overcame obstacles to reform entrenched racial prejudice, institutional inertia, and the poor education and motivation of many black enlistees. The numbers of black enlisted men increased and more and more black soldiers were assigned to integrated units; however, there was a practice among all the services to exclude African Americans from assignments to some allied nations where the U.S. had a presence. The individual services continued to limit foreign assignments for African Americans, although very seldom at the allied nations' request.

In 1949, the Marine Corps Commandant defended the USMC's segregated racial policy by arguing that the armed forces should follow society's lead in this area and not vice versa. Evidently, the Marine Corps was not aware that Jackie Robinson integrated Major League Baseball on April 15, 1947 and by 1949, a considerable number of black baseball players were in the Major Leagues. Congress began to debate more frequently the integration of the armed forced in 1949.

Senator Russell again submitted an amendment to the Selective Service Act which would have allowed servicemen to serve in segregated units if they so desired. Considered to be "the high point of the congressional fight against armed forces integration," the Russell amendment was again defeated.

The Department of Defense drafted a policy that abolished all racial quotas and established uniform draft standards. All the services were to be fully integrated by July 1, 1950. Secretary of Defense Forrestal's resignation, as well as opposition from the various service Secretaries, eventually killed this policy to establish a Service-wide racial policy.

The Army was determined to retain segregation because of senior Army leaders beliefs that blacks were unreliable and ineffective in combat and that white soldiers would not serve with African Americans.

During a news conference in October 1949, President Truman announced that his goal was the total racial integration of the U.S. Army. In March of 1950, the Secretary of the Army ordered the service to open its recruiting without regard to race.

Each of the services did everything possible to foot drag its' implementation of the Presidents' orders. During peace time, each of the services was downsizing, and this especially gave them excuses to keep only the "very best men."

Secretary of the Army Gordon Gray ordered the service to open its recruiting without regard to race. Although he got a caveat from the president that he could institute a quota if trends indicated that blacks would be disproportionately represented in the Army.

June 25, 1950 was another date that changed the American landscape. North Korean troops invaded South Korea beginning the Korean War. Within five months, the U.S. Army would double in size. Policies and practices of the armed forces would now be put to the test in this new, hot war.

During the fighting on the Korean Pusan Perimeter, several African Americans were assigned combat duties which were "the first time black servicemen were integrated as individuals in significant numbers under combat conditions." The Army began filling losses in their heretofore all white units with individuals from "a growing surplus of black replacements arriving in Japan." By early 1951, almost ten percent of all black soldiers were serving in forty-one newly integrated units.

A high ranking officer of the U.S. Eighth Army in Korea recommended that integrated units become permanent as it was successful. The integrated troops fought as a unit and there were no reports of racial friction.

In September of 1950, the 1st Marine Division was assigned numerous African-American marines, because circumstances gave them no other choice. Survival and victory on the battlefield trumped any social policy that one may have harbored during quiet peaceful times.

By March of 1951, at least half of the African Americans serving in the Marine Corps under combat conditions were assigned to integrated units. Blacks performed valiantly and were awarded decorations for valor and earned the respect of their commanders. Blacks were being accepted as part of America's Fighting Men for the first time. Despite the excellent experience in Korea, the Army located in Europe and on bases in the United States, continued to segregate their units and continued their racial quotas.

Unlike World War II, when only about 22 percent of all African Americans in the Army served in combat units, black soldiers during the Korean War were assigned to the combat branches in approximately the same percentage as white soldiers. Some of the old guard of the Army continued to cling to old sentiments and practices, but the Korean War would ultimately rewrite the outdated American paradigm.

In May of 1951, Lieutenant General Matthew B. Ridgeway, Commander of all forces in Korea, formally requested authority to abolish segregation in the Eighth Army. On the third anniversary of President Truman's order, the Army announced the full integration of its Far East Command. The integration of the U.S. Army in Korea led to greater harmony and military efficiency.

Senior Army leaders moved closer to accepting full integration. Their attitude was affected partly by the percentage of blacks in the Army by this time, and partly by the successful integration of the Eighth Army in Korea and training camps at home.

A contract study, known as PROJECT CLEAR, confirmed earlier findings that African American soldiers in integrated units fought as well as whites. Integration improved black morale and had no impact on the morale of whites. The study concluded that segregation hampered the Army's effectiveness while integration increased it.

In December of 1951, the USMC Commandant announced a general policy of racial integration and within six months, he followed up with a memo advising that the Marine Corps was now totally integrated. Mission Accomplished, but not without some issues unresolved as the Marine Corps continued to use all black stewards in Mess Halls. The Marine Corps did not assign white marines to steward duties until 1956.

By 1952, the Navy's non-white Steward's Branch was still sixty-five percent black with the remainder Filipinos. On February 1954, the navy integrated the Steward's Branch and by 1961, blacks became a minority in the Steward's Branch for the first time in thirty years.

In December 1952, the Army Chief of Staff ordered worldwide integration of this service. There was no increase in racial incidents, no breakdown in discipline, no uprising against integration by white soldiers or surrounding communities, no backlash from segregationists in Congress, or major public denouncements of the new policy.

Before the outbreak of the Korean War, the number of black American marines was about 1,500, half of whom were stewards. This number grew to 17,000 black American marines by December 1952.

According to the Project Clear Report, "As the need for more units and replacements grew during the war, newly enlisted black marines were more and more pressed into integrated service in the Far East and at home . . . The competence of these Negroes and the general absence of racial tension during their integration destroyed long accepted beliefs to the contrary and opened the way for general integration of the Marine Corps."

The last racially segregated unit in our countries armed forces ceased to exist on October 30, 1954; almost six years after President Truman ordered the Armed Services to integrate.

Nearly ninety years since the ratification of the Thirteenth Amendment to the U. S. Constitution that made black people free, they could freely join the armed services of their country, free from official discrimination or segregation.

17

The American G.I. Bill Of Rights

"FOR WHITE VETERANS ONLY"

The American G. I. Bill of Rights has been recognized as being the most successful progressive government program in the history of the United States. The Congress of the United States invested more money in education, through the G.I. Bill, for returning veterans of World War II than the government invested in the Marshall Plan, the monetary plan that resurrected Europe from the waste of the war.

Unfortunately, the American G.I Bill of Rights also served to further widen the gap between black America and white America. The G.I. Bill of Rights, formally known as "The Selective Service Readjustment Act," was signed into law a few days after the Allies invaded the European mainland on D-Day, 1944.

The forerunner to the G.I. Bill of Rights was the benefits allocated to returning servicemen after World War I. Veterans and their dependents received health care, vocational rehabilitation, disability payments and survivor benefits between 1918 and 1928. There were features of the early program that left southern politicians dissatisfied. First, the program was centralized in Washington with the creation of the Veteran's Administration. Secondly, the Veteran's Administration dealt directly with the veteran's and their families, which bypassed Congressmen. Thirdly, veteran benefits were offered directly to black veterans and their families, which resulted in a decrease in the supply of workers for domestic labor. The implementation of the World War I benefits programs created a huge lobbying organization—the American Legion.

Both the newly created Veterans Administration and the American Legion worked hand in fist to control the manner, methods and governance of the new system which evolved in the creation of the new American G.I. Bill of Rights in 1944. The principal politician who drafted the law was John Rankin of Mississippi. Representative Rankin was one of the most unashamed racists, who was openly anti-Black, anti-Jewish and anti-Catholic. Guided by the model in earlier New Deal laws, Rankin and his brethren drafted a law that left responsibility for implementation mainly to the States and localities, which, unfortunately, practiced official racism without compromise.

The principal lobbying organizations, the American Legion and the Veterans of Foreign Wars practiced segregation and were absent of any black leaders. The Veterans Administration, composed almost entirely from returned white servicemen, recommended and endorsed by the American Legion and the VFW managed hospitals that were segregated and administered housing programs that were discriminatory.

The Veterans Administration knew that legislation for veterans had to pass through powerful Southern politicians who headed most of the committees in Congress. To cultivate this support, they made clear that they were disinclined to challenge the South's race relations and enforcement of equal treatment of all veterans was non-existent.

The FDR administration attempts to centralize the management of the G.I. Bill was defeated by lobbying efforts of the American Legion and the Veterans of Foreign Wars. In a statement issued by Commander Warren Atherton of the American Legion he stated, *"We have endeavored to assure a measure of states rights in the legislation wherein control of many of the features of the bill will still rest with individual states."* In a note that he sent to his Deputy, he reinforced that the Veterans Administration had agreed not to disturb any arrangements with the South.

Jim Crow laws were still in effect and the die was cast.

There is no question in anyone's mind that the American G.I. Bill, the biggest government welfare program of all time, did more to create the American middle class than any other single event. The money on education alone through 1950 was more than was spent on the Marshall Plan. At the beginning of World War II, some 160,000 Americans were graduating from college each year. By 1949, 500,000 a year were graduating from college. By 1955, 2,250,000 veterans participated in higher education.

The USA gained more than 400,000 engineers, 200,000 teachers, 90,000 scientists, 60,000 doctors, and 22,000 dentists. Another 5,600,000 veterans enrolled in some 10,000 vocational institutions to study a whole variety of trades from carpentry to refrigeration, plumbing to electricity, automobile and airplane mechanics, to various forms of business training. For most returning soldiers, the full range of benefits—the entire cost of tuition and books plus a living stipend was relatively easy to obtain, unless you were a returning black serviceman.

The problem was not the legislation, but in the application of the legislation. Prior to 1954, the United States lived under the Plessy v. Ferguson ideology, both de jure and de facto. In the South, separate but equal was codified and in the North, separate but equal was cultural. Statistics clearly show that as many blacks as whites, proportional to their military population applied for housing and educational opportunities. For whites, the opportunity was there for the taking, and in most cases, they could attend the school of their choice and live wherever they wished.

For black returning servicemen, four of five came from the southern states. They were prohibited to attend any mainstream southern college or university. They were not permitted to attend any mainstream southern trade school. If they did learn a trade in a trade school, they were not permitted to work in that trade in the South.

Mainstream major colleges in the South were prepared to take on the surge of white servicemen returning from the war as they were funded to build more dormitories, more classrooms and homes in the area were open to white returning veterans. Black servicemen returning from military service had no such luck.

Over 55 percent of returning black servicemen applying for entry in black colleges were denied entry for lack of space or lack of housing. There was inadequate off campus housing where black students could live, nor was there extraordinary funding for additional housing on campus. Housing for married black folks was nonexistent.

The returning black servicemen had the opportunity to attend college, but the available resources in the South were lacking. The black colleges of the south were underfunded, under-resourced and were so small that they could not offer a full range of academic studies.

Fifty years after the death of Franklin Roosevelt, President Bill Clinton affectionately recalled FDR's "most enduring legacy," the American G.I. Bill of Rights. Mr. Clinton remarked that FDR's "vision most clearly embodied in the G.I. Bill . . . . which gave generations of veterans a chance to get an education, to build a strong family and good lives, and to build the nation's strongest economy ever, to change the face of America . . . . The G.I. Bill helped to unleash a prosperity never before known."

President Clinton was not alone. Many folks felt the same way that the G.I. Bill was a true social revolution that raised the entire nation to a new level and that the Bill created the American middle class. As I have discussed previously, the words are true as the Bill was probably the single most important piece of legislation to elevate America's poor to a meaningful middle class; however, it also served to widen the gap between black and white Americans.

In a study conducted by the Bureau of the Census, the Southern Regional Council, the National Urban League and the American Veterans Committee, whose active membership included Franklin Roosevelt, Jr. and Ronald Reagan, future President of the United States, observed:

> *There are two major sets of facts surrounding the life of Negro veterans in America today:*
>
> *Over a million dark-skinned ex-servicemen are, by training, discipline, sacrifice, and self-determination, prepared for integration into the nation's life as first class citizens. (2) The nation has almost universally failed to grasp the enormous opportunity which is presented through veterans' benefits for this minority group.*[80]

It was, the document concluded, "as though the G.I. Bill has been earmarked "For White Veterans Only."[81]

---

[80] Charles G. Bolte and Louis Harris, "Our Negro Veterans" (New York Public Affairs Committee, Pamphlet 128, 1947.) pg. 28.

[81] Charles G. Bolte and Louis Harris, "Our Negro Veterans" (New York Public Affairs Committee, Pamphlet 128, 1947.) pg. 20.

18

Vietnam

For the first time in our history, we fought in Vietnam as one nation, undivided. No segregation of troops—blacks and whites, together, one foxhole. The war in Vietnam was different in so many ways to any other war in our history. From the beginning, volunteers and drafted soldiers were from the entire community, without regard to race.

The soldiers who eventually made it to the front lines have long been a subject of controversy as I will explain. It appeared to many that the casualty rate of minorities and the poor and under-educated were disproportionately over represented in Vietnam.

Appearances may have been accurate. There is some truth to this, but it will be instructive to discuss the why of the data.

World War II was "the Good War," clear of purpose, and universally seen by all Americans as a war of Good versus Evil. Hollywood portrayed our armies to be totally homogenous, with no class or racial distinctions. America drew on every segment of society. That foxhole that John Wayne held on *The Sands of Iwo Jima* included a guy from Brooklyn and a guy named Rodriguez or was that *Battleground* with Van Johnson? We felt good about our boys fighting the Nazis. They were us!

Members from every segment of the American population were drafted or volunteered and all served and died equally—although most blacks died separately. But there was an unseen distinction that slowly weaved its way into the newly developing "caste system" of America that separated the ultra educated and the not so educated.

In many respects, by choice and by government design, the ultra educated withdrew from military service in substantial proportions. There were many exceptions to this among young men who joined the Navy and the Air Force, but for those who served on the front lines of Vietnam, it was a war of our poor under-educated folks against the enemy.

The war was an unpopular war, and it would have been more unpopular if the sons of the educationally advantaged and influential Americans would have been drafted and sent to the front lines. Congress and President Johnson protected our college bound, educated young men by exempting them from the draft.

A college deferment was relatively easy to get. A prospect for the armed services must have been college bound, or enrolled in graduate or post graduate work. If they met those qualifications, they were not drafted and were not sent to Vietnam. The young men who went, fought and died, were from our not so educated class, the poor who could not afford college and the young men who had no interest in college. It was estimated that no more than ten percent of enlisted men in combat units had some college experience and less than one percent were college graduates.

Upon enlistment or being drafted, recruits were given aptitude tests and the results were categorized into four levels. The highest grades were assigned to further education as specialists, or immediately to technical positions. The lowest grades were slotted into combat positions. Ninety three percent of black recruits scored in the lower levels of the qualification tests and were therefore assigned to combat units of the Army and the Marine Corps.

The results of the assignments essentially set a predetermined high casualty rate among black Americans. In 1965 through 1966, black casualties in Vietnam was over 20 percent of the total casualty rate, although black Americans were only eleven percent of our Vietnam force.

Black leaders in America were not insensitive to the numbers as so many black youngsters were coming home in coffins, and it appeared, at a higher rate than should have been expected. After the data was verified, they sought the attention of the President of the United States and subsequently, President Johnson ordered that black participation be cut back. As a result, the black casualty rate was reduced to almost twelve percent by 1969.

"Overall, of all enlisted men who died in Viet Nam, African Americans made up 14.1% of the total."[82]

In the irony of ironies, after a century of denying a quality education to blacks in the South, and in many cases, denying education to poor whites, the South experienced

---

[82] William F. Abbott, Vietnam Veteran, americanwarlibrary.com. retrieved 9/20/2007

the greatest number of soldiers killed in Vietnam. Nearly thirty-four percent of the war dead in Vietnam came from the South.

The reasons were maybe threefold: (1) The South was home to 53 percent of all blacks living in the United States, (2) the South had the poorest educational systems in the country and (3) plain old patriotism. The South was home to many young men from small towns with a family tradition of fighting in wars and would not think of trying to avoid this, or any other war.

"Asking for a Draft deferment was a reprehensible idea for these products of the old Confederacy, whose fathers, grandfathers, uncles and other ancestors had fought in all the wars of this country."[83]

The most precise definition of who died and who lived in the Vietnam War was that the college bound stayed at home while the non-college bound served and died. The lower the test scores on the Armed Forces Qualification Test, the higher the chance of dying. Education was the great equalizer in the Vietnam War.

---

[83] William F. Abbott, Vietnam Veteran, americanwarlibrary.com. retrieved 9/20/2007

19

Robeson To Robinson

The 20th Century brought new challenges to America's black citizens who began making extraordinary contributions to American culture. Scott Joplin, a black man from East Texas born a freeman in 1867, introduced America to Ragtime. W.C. Handy, born in 1873 in Florence, Alabama, introduced the Blues to America. The truly original American music comes from Negro music—Jazz, Ragtime, and the Blues—all originating from black gentlemen from the New South.

Jack Johnson, a black man born in Galveston, Texas to former slaves in 1878, became the Heavyweight Champion of the World from 1908 to 1915. The story of Jack Johnson is well known, and we won't dwell too much on his history with the following exception. The *crimes* Jack Johnson was convicted of had to do with cohabitating with white women, a crime of great significance to white America.

The Mann Act of 1910 was used by the Justice Department to curtail commercialized vice. It was often used to prosecute persons who did not conform to conventional morality. Over the years, charges of Mann Act violations were leveled against architect Frank Lloyd Wright, the actor Charlie Chaplin, Rock and Roll legend Chuck Berry and Heavyweight Champion Jack Johnson. Of these four, only Berry and Johnson were convicted of a Mann Act violation. Both Berry and Johnson were black.

Most everyone knows the story of Jack Roosevelt Robinson, the first black man to play in the Major Leagues. Jackie Robinson's achievements are legendary and the barriers he had to overcome are well documented and known so well a retelling will not add materially to this book; however, the story of Paul Robeson is not as well known, and it is his story that will accentuate the issues of segregation and discrimination, and the effects to our country when talent is wasted through ignorance and malice.

In 1996, I attended a lobby reception for the play, "*Mr. Rickey Calls a Meeting,*" which was a theatrical production of the signing of Jackie Robinson to a professional baseball contract. The characters in the play were Mr. Branch Rickey, Jackie Robinson, Joe Lewis, Bojangles and Paul Robeson. Bojangles, Lewis and Robeson were Jackie Robinson's advisors. The host of the lobby reception discussed the play before we witnessed it and told of each character. In describing Paul Robeson, she asked if anyone knew who Paul Robeson was and a gentleman in the audience said, "Paul Robeson was a communist!" "That's right," she said.

To sum up Paul Robeson as a communist is to sum up Pablo Picasso as a socialist. The description is not only inaccurate, it is infantile and degrading.

Paul Robeson was born in Princeton, New Jersey, the son of William Drew Robeson, a runaway slave who eventually graduated from Lincoln College in 1878. Attending a fully integrated high school, Paul Robeson took the familiar courses of the day; debate, oratory, literature and mathematics and excelled in athletics. In his senior year in high school, Robeson placed first in a competitive examination for scholarships to enter Rutgers University in 1915.

Paul Robeson became an excellent student-athlete at Rutgers and was a rarity, even by today's standards. He was named to Walter Camp's All American Football team in 1917 and 1918 and was named Rutgers University class valedictorian in 1919. Robeson earned fifteen varsity letters, was a member of the prestigious Phi Beta Kappa Society and the Cap and Skull Society of Rutgers.

Robeson was a pioneer in the professional football ranks and played long enough to pay his way through Columbia Law School, where he earned his law degree. He was hired by a law firm in New York, but soon became disenchanted and quit, as among other incidents, secretaries would not take dictation from a black man.

Paul Robeson was truly a Renaissance man. He spoke numerous languages and was an outstanding singer, and he sang in many languages. He made his career as a successful entertainer in America and Europe. Here was a man that could have been anything, in today's' America; however, he was a black man in the early part of the 20th Century.

Frustrated at the lack of opportunities in the business world and not being able to perform in concerts in all parts of the United States, Robeson found his niche in Europe, where he was accepted for what he was; that is, a truly remarkable gentleman and entertainer. Robeson, with his legal background, began to speak about his experiences in America and about the lot of black people in America.

The foreign press picked up on his comments and they were re-printed in U.S. newspapers. This was the 1920s, when many leftists in America were looking at the new Soviet Union as a people's paradise. Robeson made the comments that forever labeled him. He was quoted as saying that American blacks would not take up arms against Russia, as he saw the USSR more compatible with his sense of equality for all citizens.

His remarks were similar to the remarks of another black man, Muhammad Ali, almost 50 years later, that, "I ain't got no quarrel with them Viet Cong... They never called me nigger."

Have Robeson's remarks been distorted and taken out of context? It matters not, as his reputation was forever frozen in time, as the young hostess said in Sacramento in 1997, "Paul Robeson was a communist!"

An incredible backlash against Robeson occurred in the United States, and as has been our wont, we rioted when he returned to perform in concerts in the United States. By 1950, Robeson was so detested by Americans that the State Department revoked his visa, unless he would agree not to make political speeches. So much for free speech.

The great Jackie Robinson, now in his third year in Major League baseball, had become all that white people expected from a black man. Jackie Robinson was an Army veteran and although subjected to brutal racism, he had kept his mouth shut and just did his job. He was equally as articulate as Robeson and because of this was asked by the House Un-American Activities Committee to address Paul Robeson's assertions.

"Seated before the House committee, the Dodger star strongly denounced American racial policies. '*I'm not fooled because I've had a chance open to very few Negro Americans,*' stated Robinson. He vowed to continue fighting racial discrimination in sports and other areas. At the same time, Robinson rejected Robeson's assertion that blacks would not fight for the United States. '*I've got too much invested for my wife and child and myself in the future of this country, and I and other Americans of many races and faiths have too much invested in our country's welfare, for any of us to throw it away for a siren song sung in bass,*' the Dodger star testified."[84]

"Newspapers lavished praise on Robinson, emphasizing his denunciation of Robeson and the Communists and downplaying other parts of his speech. The episode greatly enhanced Robinson's popularity. Nonetheless, it remained one of the more embarrassing moments of his life. Robinson's attack on Robeson contributed to the pillorying and banishment of one of the most talented figures in American history. Shortly before his death, Robinson defended the contents of his

---

[84] Jules Tygiel, *Baseball's Great Experiment,* page 334. 1983

1949 speech but added, 'I have grown wiser and closer to the painful truth about America's destructiveness. And, I do have an increased respect for Paul Robeson, who . . . . sacrificed himself, his career, and the wealth and comfort he once enjoyed because, I believe, he was sincerely trying to help his people.'"[85]

During the McCarthy era of the 1950s, every attempt was made to silence and discredit Robeson because of his political views and dedication to civil rights. In 1958, he won his passport battle with the government and traveled to Europe where he was showered with awards and played to packed houses. He returned to the United States, never again to entertain on stage and lived in seclusion for the last 10 years of his life and died in 1976, two hundred years after the Declaration of Independence which proudly proclaimed "*all men are created equal.*"

---

[85] Jules Tygiel, *Baseball's Great Experiment,* page 334. 1983

20

Black Hard Times

The Great Depression, beginning in 1929 and ending when America entered World War II was an era known today as "Hard Times." This period of American history is well chronicled in books and movies, the most famous being "The Grapes of Wrath" chronicling the lives of the Joad family of Oklahoma migrating to California in the early 1930s. The story describes the hardships of the "Okies" trying to survive in the California farm country.

Other books and movies covering the era are mostly about the gangsters that sprang up in the Midwest and Southwest that have become American folklore. In the years 1930 to 1936, gangsters like Alvin Karpus, Bonnie and Clyde, John Dillinger, Machine Gun Kelly, Pretty Boy Floyd, Baby Face Nelson, and the Ma Barker gang robbed banks and committed more serious crimes. They were pursued by the newly created FBI and were covered extensively by the print and movie media. In many cases, the movies glorified the exploits and virtues of the gangsters, much as they did with the story of Jesse James. After all, the gangs were only stealing from the *"enemy"*—banks and railroads.

As many books that I have read about this era in American history, I could not find one that chronicled the lives of Black Americans. Four out of five Black Americans still lived in the "Old South;" however, the migration to the Midwest and West was beginning. Their story during this period can be found between the pages of more detailed books about the plight of white Americans.

There is a great deal of information about the hardships of white Americans and very little about black Americans, but one can imagine that as hard as times were for whites, they were tenfold tougher on blacks. It was not uncommon for cities, like Dallas, Texas, to post notices that the charity available to whites during the Great Depression was not available to blacks.

There is ample evidence that the white gangs that roamed the Southwest and Midwest were terrorists, or should have been so branded, but as in the times of Jesse James, they were not. They lived quite comfortably among their "own kind." I could not find stories of comparable black gangs as the white Dillinger gangs, or their contemporaries. I could only imagine the ramifications to the black communities if such gangs were black and were robbing and looting as so many white gangs were robbing and looting throughout the Southwest and Midwest.

One just has to read about the race riots of Springfield, Illinois, in 1908 where it was alleged that a black man had sexually assaulted a white woman. After three days of rioting, where black businesses were destroyed and six people were killed, liberal white men were shocked at the carnage and hate manifested against the black community in the hometown of Abraham Lincoln. They met in New York City later that year, and along with prominent black citizens, formed the National Association for the Advancement Colored People (NAACP), to "promote equality of rights and eradicate caste or race prejudice . . ."

The Tulsa race riots of 1921 were becoming the norm. A rumored rape of a white girl by a black man was the ignition that began riots and ended in murder and destruction of property. The murder was almost always of black people and the destruction of property was almost always in black communities.

I could not find a race riot where allegedly a white man had raped a black girl, and blacks then murdered whites and destroyed white property in white communities.

The root cause of the Tulsa riots was that a white girl had charged a black youth with attempted rape. The black youth was arrested and placed in a local jail. There were rumors of a lynching by white folk, so a contingent of black men came to the jail to protect the black youngster.

"There was a confrontation at the jail and a mob numbering more than ten thousand attacked the black community. Automatic weapons were brought into use; eight airplanes were deployed to spy on the movements of the black people and were used to bomb the colored section of town."[86]

Four companies of the National Guard were deployed to stop the rioting, but not until fifty whites and over 300 Blacks were killed making the Tulsa riots the worst in American history.

---

[86] The Negro Holocaust: Lynching and Race Riots in the United States, 1880-1950. Robert A. Gibson.

"The summer of 1919, called "The Red Summer" by James Weldon Johnson, ushered in the greatest period of interracial violence the nation had ever witnessed. During the summer there were twenty-six race riots in such cities as Chicago, Illinois; Washington, D.C.; Elaine, Arkansas; Charleston, South Carolina; Knoxville and Nashville, Tennessee; Longview, Texas; and Omaha, Nebraska. More than one hundred Blacks were killed in these riots and thousands were wounded and left homeless." [87]

"Race riots were caused by a great number of social, political and economic factors. Joseph Boskin, author of *Urban Racial Violence* observed that there were certain general patterns in the major twentieth century riots:"[88]

1. "In each of the race riots, with few exceptions, it was white people that sparked the incident by attacking Black people.

2. In the majority of the riots, some extraordinary social condition prevailed at the time of the riot; prewar social changes, wartime mobility, post-war adjustment, or economic depression.

3. The majority of the riots occurred during the hot summer months.

4. Rumor played an extremely important role in causing many riots. Rumors of some criminal activity by Blacks against whites perpetuated the actions of white mobs.

5. The police force, more than any other institution, was invariably involved as a precipitating cause or perpetuating factor in the riots. In almost every one of the riots, the police sided with the attackers, either by actually participating in, or by failing to quell the attack.

6. In almost every instance, the fighting occurred within the Black community."[89]

One can only imagine what would have been the reaction of the state and federal governments, local governments and citizens, if Dillinger, Karpus, Pretty Boy Floyd, Bonnie and Clyde or Baby Face Nelson had all been black. Wholesale destruction of black communities when there was a rumor of a crime was not an uncommon event.

---

[87] The Negro Holocaust: Lynching and Race Riots in the United States, 1880-1950. Robert A. Gibson.

[88] Retrieved from the archives of Ferris State University, JIM CROW Museum of Racist Memorbilia. Retrieved August 21, 2007

[89] Joseph Boskin, Urban Racial Violence, Beverly Hills, 1976, pp 14-15 retrieved www.ferris.edu/jimcrow/what.htm retrieved 8/21/2007

I believe there would have been the wholesale slaughter of the guilty and innocents in the pursuit of justice.

In drafting the constitution for Oklahoma's application to become a new state in 1906, a young Texas transplant, William Henry David Murray and his allies included explicit white supremacist and segregationist clauses similar to Texas's Reconstruction laws, which had institutionalized segregation forty years before. The Texas Reconstruction Laws forbade blacks from working any job in Texas save as field hands. The application for Oklahoma statehood was submitted to the United States Congress and was rejected. Theodore Roosevelt objected to these clauses and had them withdrawn and Oklahoma was admitted to the Union in 1907.

William Henry David Murray was elected Governor of Oklahoma in 1930 on a campaign slogan of "The Three C's—Corporations, Carpetbaggers and Coons . . . . Blacks were inferior to whites in every way, Murray said, and must be fenced from society like quarantined hogs."[90]

In 1972, the Oklahoma State Legislature changed the name of a state college to Murray State College in honor of their former governor. Bigotry and racism has never been a disqualifier in naming public buildings, parks or schools after folks who have otherwise contributed to society.

During the Great Depression and accompanying Dust Bowl periods, the state and charities did all they could to feed, clothe and medicate the people, except for black persons. After Franklin Roosevelt and the "New Deal" were introduced, folks were getting some relief from the Federal Government. Soup lines and work paid for by the Federal government became a mainstay of life in the United States after 1932, and the Federal Government became the employer of first resort until World War II when the great military industrial business became the engine that took America out of the Great Depression. But like many government programs, the implementation was local and local meant whites first or whites only.

More than 2 million people found government jobs that paid a minimum of $12.00 a week, but nearly 25 million were still without work depending on charity, part-time jobs, or black market income (moonshine, etc.) or in some cases, robbing banks.

"For Black Americans the unemployment rate was 50 percent. Throughout the South and in some places in the North, notes were posted on job sites that read,

---

[90] Timothy Egan. *THE WORST HARD TIMES, The untold story of those who survived the Great American Dust Bowl.* A Mariner Book, Houghton Mifflin Company, Boston-New York. Pg.109

"No jobs for niggers until every white man has a job." It took an Executive Order from FDR in May 1935 to open up the public works ranks for all races."[91]

"The sign at the edge of Dalhart, Texas— "BLACK MAN DON'T LET THE SUN GO DOWN ON YOU HERE" was strictly enforced. In February (1933), a norther came through the High Plains, sending the mercury plummeting to seven degrees. The hazy, arctic air hung on for a week. When two black men got off the train in Dalhart, hungry and nearly hypothermic, they looked around for something to eat and a place to get warm. They found a door open in a shed at the train depot. Inside was some food and shelter from a cold so painful it burned their hands and feet like a blowtorch.

'Two Negroes Arrested': the Dalhart Texan reported how the men, aged nineteen and twenty-three, had sniffed around the train station, looking for food. They were cuffed, locked up in the county jail, and after a week brought out for arraignment before a justice of the peace, Hugh Edwards. The judge ordered the men to dance. The men hesitated; this was supposed to be a bond hearing. The railroad agent said these men were good for nothing but negro-toe tapping. The judge smiled; he said he wanted to see it.

'Tap dance,' Edwards told the men.

'Here?'

'Yes. Before the court.'

The men started to dance, forced silly grins on their faces, reluctant. After the tap dance, the judge banged his gavel and ordered the men back to jail for another two months."[92]

The Great Depression, "Hard Times," lasted from 1929 through the beginning of World War II in 1941 when the government accelerated our industrial output through spending on our war machine. Black hard times continued as jobs were still difficult to get.

---

[91] THE WORST HARD TIMES, "The untold story of those who survived the Great American Dust Bowl," Timothy Egan. A Mariner Book, Houghton Mifflin Company, Boston-New York. Pg. 227

[92] THE WORST HARD TIMES, "The untold story of those who survived the Great American Dust Bowl," Timothy Egan. A Mariner Book, Houghton Mifflin Company, Boston-New York. Pgs. 176-177

21

Segregation Now, Segregation Forever

Each war where Americans fought, the Spanish-American War, World War I and II, the Korean War and the war in Vietnam, expanded the world view of black servicemen that would be useful in the years ahead. Returning to America after each war, blacks remained more unsatisfied with their lot, however, segregation was the continuous norm in America

"Schools, churches, restaurants, hospitals were separated from the inception after the Civil War. Cities separated cemeteries and parks and Counties segregated court houses. In 1885, a Memphis newspaper described how thoroughly the races were separated: *'The colored people make no effort to obtrude themselves upon the whites in the public schools, their churches, their fairs, their Sunday-schools, their picnics, their social parties, hotels or banquets. They prefer their own preachers, teachers, schools, picnics, hotels and social gatherings.'* In the countryside as well as in town, blacks and whites associated with members of their own race except in those situations associated when interracial association could not be avoided, commerce, work, politics and travel."[93]

In other words, blacks were *happy*. It is not the first time that whites explained the feelings on behalf of blacks, and each time there was ample evidence that the explanations were self-serving. Most whites welcomed segregation in general; however, many "troublemaking" blacks fought against the new laws with boycotts, lawsuits, and complaints, many saw no use in fighting inasmuch as whites had the political power and fighting white benefactors made little sense, nor did it make sense to make new enemies among the whites.

What was it like to be black in Jim Crow America?

My brothers and I are second generation Americans, parents born in Arizona and New Mexico and who raised us in California ingrained with the belief that "we could

---

[93] Edward L. Ayers. *The Promise of the New South*, page 136.

be all we could be." My friend, Harold, a black man, was born in Memphis, Tennessee in 1938, whose family lived in the South "forever." He went to a segregated high school, attended Tuskegee Institute, and earned a college degree. Harold worked for the Postal Service in Memphis as a letter carrier with little opportunity to rise beyond a letter carrier's lot.

Harold's life experience included the knowledge that his grandfather, after a dispute with a white neighbor over the use of a mule, was lynched, dragged behind a truck, and whose body was dumped on the front yard of Harold's grandmother. As far as Harold knows, no one was ever prosecuted for his grandfather's death.

Harold and I both graduated from high school in 1956. In 1956, I was not aware of the significance of *Brown vs. Board of Education (1954) n*or had ever heard of Emmett Till (1955). Harold lived the 50's rather different than I did.

What was it like to be a black man in the segregated South? Let me suggest some of the "rules" Harold's grandfather, father and he had to adjust to in Jim Crow America.

The following material was extrapolated from the works of Stetson Kennedy, born in 1916 in Jacksonville, Florida from his book, "The Jim Crow Guide: The Way it Was Before the Overcoming."

Normally, I will write what I have learned from a source, but no one can paraphrase or simulate the writings of Stetson Kennedy and I did not attempt to do so. The words are too powerful for me to attempt to improve upon.

- "A Black male could not offer his hand (to shake hands) with a White male because it implied being socially equal. Obviously a Black male could not offer his hand or any other part of his body to a White woman, because he risked being accused of rape."

- "Blacks and Whites were not supposed to eat together. If they did eat together, Whites were to be served first, and some sort of partition was to be placed between them."

- "Under no circumstances was a black male to offer to light the cigarette of a White female—that gesture implied intimacy."

- "Blacks were not allowed to show public affection toward one another in public, especially kissing, because it offended Whites."

- "Jim Crow etiquette prescribed that Blacks were introduced to Whites, never Whites to Blacks. For example: "Mr. Peters (the White person), this is Charlie (the Black person), that I spoke to you about.""

- "Whites did not use courtesy titles of respect when referring to Blacks, for example, Mr., Mrs., Miss., Sir., or Ma'am,. Instead Blacks were called by their first names. Blacks had to use courtesy titles when referring to Whites, and were not allowed to call them by their first names."

- "If a white man did not know the name of a black man, he simply referred to him as Boy or Uncle for older black men. If a black man did not know the name of a white man, and when he was spoken to first, he referred to the white man as Sir!"

- "If a Black person rode in a car driven by a White person, the Black person sat in the back seat, or the back of a truck."

- "When boarding a bus, blacks rode in the back rows. They paid their fares in the front and if there were white folks on the bus, they left the bus, and reentered through the back door. It was not uncommon that, after payment, and when they left the bus and before reentering, the bus driver would leave without the fare payer."

- "In buses that were full, there had to be an empty row between blacks and whites, for fear that black knees might touch white women knees, then the blacks had to stand in the back or leave the bus, rather than sit in the empty rows."

- "Black men removed their hats in public places inhabited by whites, and white men did not remove their hats even while in a black home."

- "Never assert or even intimate that a White person is lying."

- "Never impute dishonorable intentions to a White person."

- "Never suggest that a White person is from an inferior class"

- "Never lay claim to, or overly demonstrate, superior knowledge or intelligence."

- "Never curse a White person"

- "Never laugh derisively at a White person"

- "Never comment upon the appearance of a White female."[94]

I first met Harold Wilson in 1982 and have worked closely and socialized with him and his family. I am a witness that he has broken every one of the above "rules" tenfold since he has lived in California.

---

[94] *Stetson Kennedy, "Jim Crow Guide: The Way It Was." Boca Raton: Florida University Press, Florida Atlantic University*, retrieved 08/21/2007

22

Integration Now, Integration Forever

The 1950s were a peaceful period in America with the indifference of the North and the Jim Crow laws and culture of the South. I had no idea in 1947 that blacks were not playing baseball in the big leagues and we had no idea that black children could not go to school with white children in most of the South and Midwest. We grew up in integrated California, where certainly discrimination existed, but not obvious segregation.

We followed the baseball big leagues on radio and newspapers, and with very few pictures; we were totally ignorant of the outside world. When *Brown v. Board of Education* was decided in 1954 by the Supreme Court, it was a newspaper story in my community and that was about it. Little did we know that *Brown* was the beginning of the 1960s. The era of protests and the Vietnam War, the 1968 Democratic National Convention and the Civil Rights movement that awakened America through television.

Brown v. Board of Education eliminated Plessy v. Ferguson and Separate but Equal as national policy. There would be no living in parallel universes for blacks and whites; it would be *"One Nation, Under God" with all deliberate speed*. Some have said that *Brown* was the Second Reconstruction, but how far back was black society after almost a century of overt discrimination and pit stops through numerous obstacles?

Brown opened up the myriad of cases that overturned centuries of officially sanctioned racial segregation in education, housing and employment. Chief Justice Earl Warren, former Governor of California became the hero of the progressive elements of our society.

It was no secret what conservative America thought of Mr. Warren; one just had to travel in the Central Valley of California to see all the "IMPEACH EARL WARREN" signs that lined the major state highways dissecting California north and south.

What did blacks want that so infuriated the conservative elements of our society? They wanted to attend good schools, live in better neighborhoods, be exposed to better medical facilities, and acquire better employment and to become an equal member of our society. Was it too much to ask for? Apparently it was because change was resisted at every opportunity. Whites theorized that for every good job given to a black man, there was one less job for a white man. It was a zero sum game, blacks get a job, whites lose a job.

When the Supreme Court overturned *Plessy*, all thought that within a reasonable amount of time, black children and white children would attend grade schools and high schools together almost immediately. Furthermore, they believed that blacks would be admitted in colleges of their choice when they qualified under the requirements of the schools.

Not so. The South interpreted the Court's order to integrate *"by all deliberate speed"* to mean, as Justice Thurgood Marshall later said, "SLOW!" Ten years after Brown, Southern states, where most blacks lived, had not achieved even one-percent integration with whites in public schools. The busing of school children became a remedy established by progressive courts to correct the inaction of the States, and busing became a national argument.

Much of the South dragged their feet to accommodate black children from entering schools, the most well known was Little Rock's Central High School in 1957, my first year of college. Television brought us the pictures from Little Rock of Governor Orval Faubus defying a Federal court order on the basis of States Rights and Federalism. We witnessed Federal troops policing on domestic soil, 90 years after Reconstruction and the Posse Comitatus law of 1878, forbidding Federal troops conducting police actions on American soil.

President Dwight Eisenhower is given much credit for his sending the 101st Airborne Division to Little Rock; however, history has surely disclosed that he did it reluctantly. Eisenhower, on the eve of the *Brown* decision had a private meeting with Chief Justice Earl Warren at the White House, where he told Warren, "The Southern States were full of good will and good intentions . . . These are not bad people," the president said, "all they are concerned about is to see that their sweet little girls are not required to sit in school alongside some big buck." Chief Justice Warren never forgave Eisenhower for that crude and stupid remark.[95]

---

[95] Jim Newton. *"Justice for All, Earl Warren and the Nation he Made,"* page 315

Eisenhower never actively supported, nor blessed the *Brown* decision and, in fact, once called Earl Warren one of the biggest mistakes he had ever made. The bully pulpit was never used by the Eisenhower Administration to advance the ideals of *Brown*.

On television, magazines and newspapers we witnessed white citizens yelling obscenities at innocent black children just trying to go to school, and we didn't understand. We certainly didn't feel the ugliness of segregation until we learned later the story of Emmitt Till. Blacks in Chicago, Detroit, Los Angeles and New York were not as impacted by segregation as their brethren in the South and in many ways they were indifferent as long as their lives were relatively untouched, but Emmitt Till changed all of black society, as well as the conscience of white society.

23

The Murder of Emmett Till

The story of Emmett Till, even to this day boggles the imagination. How could this event ever happen in the United States?

Emmett Till, a 14 year old boy from Chicago, Illinois traveled to Money, Mississippi in 1955 to visit his cousins. In 1955, I was a 15 year old junior at Coachella Valley Union High School, in Thermal, California along with my friend Clay Tribble.

Harold Wilson was a junior at Hamilton High School in Memphis, Tennessee. He remembers quite vividly the circumstances surrounding Emmett Till. I have no recollection about the events and as far as I can recall, the murder of Emmett Till was not a conversation piece in Southern California among high school kids.

Emmett Till, this audacious boy from Chicago was showing off to his cousins in Mississippi that he was not afraid of white people. He probably boasted that he knew plenty of white folks in Chicago, and white girls too. He showed his cousins that he was not afraid following a white lady into a General Store in Money, Mississippi.

My guess is that he strutted into the store behind the white lady with a smile on his face and he eventually bought some candy. As he was leaving the store, he smiled at the white lady and said, "Bye, Baby." The woman was Carolyn Bryant, the wife of the store owner.

I suppose Emmett then boasted to his southern cousins about his flirting and told them, "See, I am not afraid." The cousins and Emmett went about their business and eventually went home and soon forgot about the event.

A few days later, in the dead of night, two white men entered the cabin where Emmitt was staying with his Uncle, Mose Wright, and snatched Emmitt from the cabin and drove off with him.

Emmett's kidnappers were Roy Bryant, the owner of the store and husband of Carolyn Bryant, and J.W. Milam, his brother-in-law.

Three days later, Emmitt Till's body was found in the Tallahatchie River. One eye was gouged out, and his head crushed in and a bullet shattered his skull. It was almost impossible to identify the body as being Emmitt Till. The uncle, Mose Wright, identified the body by recognizing the ring Emmitt had been wearing.

By all local reports, the entire community, both black and white, was horrified by the crime and had arrested both Bryant and Milam for kidnapping. The local newspapers and white officials reported that all "decent" people were disgusted with the murder and declared that justice would be done.

The body of Emmitt Till was shipped back to Chicago, where his mother, Mamie Bradley still resided. When it arrived, Mrs. Bradley inspected it carefully to ensure that it really was her son. Then, she insisted on an open-casket funeral, so that "all the world could see what they did to my son." Over four days, thousands of people saw Emmett's body. Many more blacks across the country who might not have otherwise heard of the case were shocked by pictures that appeared in JET Magazine, the magazine that marketed itself to the national black population.

America reacted in different ways. Many saw the Emmett Till case as a "Southern Problem," or as a "Mississippi Problem," only. Even blacks outside the South, shocked as they were, only screamed for justice in Mississippi, and did not, at the onset, condemn the entire South.

If folks in Mississippi, who were just as horrified as every other mature adult in this country, would have done the right thing, history would not have turned as it did. When the national print media turned their spotlight on Mississippi, local white folks defended "their way of life," and resented being labeled as backwards and racists.

When the defendants, Roy Bryant and J.W. Milam, were unable to secure counsel at the onset, five prominent local lawyers stepped forward to defend them and the same city officials who had at first condemned the murders began supporting them.

The trial began in a segregated courthouse in Sumner, Mississippi on September 19, 1955. The prosecution had trouble finding witnesses willing to testify against the two men. At that time in Mississippi, it was unheard of for a black person to publicly accuse a white person of committing a crime.

The chief witness for the prosecution was Emmett's sixty-four year old uncle Mose Wright. When asked if he could point out the men who had taken his nephew that dark summer night, he stood, pointed to Milam and Bryant, and said "Dar he"—"There he is." Wright's bravery encouraged other blacks to testify against the two defendants. All had to be hurried out of the state after their testimony.

In the end, however, even the incredible courage of these blacks did not make a difference. Defense attorney John C. Whitten told the jurors in his closing statement, "Your fathers will turn over in their graves if Milam and Bryant are found guilty and I'm sure that every last Anglo-Saxon one of you has the courage to free these men in the face of that outside pressure." The jurors listened to him. They deliberated for just over an hour, and then returned a "not guilty" verdict on September 23rd. The jury foreman later explained, "I feel the state failed to prove the identity of the body."

The impact of the Emmett Till case on black America was even greater than that of the *Brown vs. Board of Education* decision. For the first time, northern blacks saw that violence against blacks in the South could affect them in the North. In Mamie Bradley's words, "Two months ago I had a nice apartment in Chicago. I had a good job. I had a son. When something happened to the Negroes in the South I said, 'That's their business, not mine.' Now I know how wrong I was. The murder of my son has shown me that what happens to any of us, anywhere in the world, had better be the business of us all." Blacks, in the North as well as in the South, would not easily forget the murder of Emmett Till.[96]

The murder of Emmitt Till created outrage in Europe and in the Middle East where newspapers extensively covered the funeral in Chicago, where over 50,000 people attended. According to an extensive survey of newspapers in six European and North African countries by the American Jewish Committee, the outrage was unanimous and damaged the reputation of the United States.

I am happy to report that my home town newspaper, the Indio Date Palm, also took umbrage when its' editor, Ward H. Grant, wrote on September 29, 1955 the following opinion piece in his column, *STRICTLY PERSONAL*.

> *"We're not from Mississippi, but if we were we'd be ashamed to admit it after the display of bigotry, prejudice and inhumanity that marked the "fixed" trial of Roy Bryant and J.W. Milam, the Mississippi hot shots who kidnapped, beat and murdered a 14 year old colored boy for assertedly whistling at Bryant's wife. As people familiar with the stinking prejudiced politics of Mississippi predicted, the men were completely exonerated. We don't doubt that the boy whistled. Any city boy, regardless of color or nationality, visiting country relatives just automatically becomes a "show off." The abnormality was not on the boy's part, it was on the part*

---

[96] Lisa Cozzens (lisa@www.watson.org. retrieved 08/20/2007

of the bird-brained Mississipians whom we are not at all happy to think of as fellow citizens of the United States. And we don't think much of the newspapers in the area, either, for permitting such mockery of justice."

Harold Wilson remembers the Emmett Till events as if they happened last week. He remembers the chills of the moment and the terror he and his classmates felt. Unlike other times, there was no rioting in the streets of Memphis or any other city in the South. The expectation that something like this could happen was not a surprise to black folks who lived in the South, but the event woke up their brethren, and supporters, in other parts of America.

The case of Emmitt Till in 1955 was prologue. The Civil Rights movement, which heretofore, was a mix of marches and sit-ins, with a court case or two thrown in, now took on a more feverish pitch. This case, and other similar injustices, became nightly fodder in the new media, television, that had just began taking hold throughout America.

The Civil Rights Memorial in Montgomery, Alabama lists the many names martyred during the Civil Rights era of 1954 to 1968.

1955: Belzoni, Mississippi: **Rev. George Wesley Lee**, *an NAACP leader and one of the first black people registered to vote in Humphreys County, used his pulpit and his printing press to urge others to vote. White officials offered Lee protection on the condition he remove his name from the list of registered voters and end his voter registration efforts, but Lee refused and was murdered.*

1955: Brookhaven, Mississippi: **Lamar Smith** *was shot dead on the courthouse lawn by a white man in broad daylight while dozens of people watched. The killer was never indicted because no one would admit they saw a white man shoot a black man. Smith had organized blacks to vote in a recent election.*

1955: Mayflower, Texas: **John Earl Reese**, *16, was dancing in a café when white men fired shots into the windows. Reese was killed and two others wounded. The shootings were part of an attempt by whites to terrorize blacks into giving up plans for a new school.*

1957: Montgomery, Alabama: **Willie Edwards, Jr.**, *a truck driver, was on his way to work when he was stopped by four Klansmen. The men thought Edwards was another man who they believed was dating a white woman. They forced Edwards at gunpoint to jump off a bridge into the Alabama River. Edwards' body was found three months later.*

1959: Poplarville, Mississippi: **Mack Charles Parker,** *23, was accused of raping a white woman. Three days before his case was set for trial, a masked mob took him from his jail cell, beat him, shot him, and threw him in the Pearl River.*

1961: Liberty, Mississippi: **Herbert Lee,** *who worked with civil rights leader Bob Moses to help register black voters, was killed by a state legislator, who claimed self-defense and was never arrested.* **Louis Allen,** *a black man who witnessed the murder, was later also killed.*

1963: Attalla, Alabama: **William Lewis Moore,** *35, former World War II Marine, letter carrier, from Baltimore, Maryland, was shot and killed during a one-man protest march against segregation. Moore, a white man, had planned to deliver a letter to the governor of Mississippi urging the end to segregation when he was shot and killed.*

1963: Jackson, Mississippi: **Medgar Evers,** *was directing NAACP operations in Mississippi, was leading a campaign for integration in Jackson when he was shot and killed by a sniper at the doorstep of his home.*

September 15, 1963: Birmingham, Alabama: **Addie Mae Collins, Denise McNair, Carole Robertson, and Cynthia Wesley** *were getting ready for church services when a bomb exploded at the Sixteenth Street Baptist Church, killing all four of the school age children. The church had been a center for civil rights meetings and marches.*

September 15, 1963: Birmingham, Alabama: **Virgil Lamar Ware,** *13, was riding on the handlebars of his brother's bicycle when he was fatally shot by white teenagers. The white youths had come from a segregationist rally held in the aftermath of the Sixteenth Street Baptist Church bombing.*

1964: Liberty, Mississippi: **Louis Allen,** *who witnessed the murder of civil rights worker Herbert Lee, endured years of threats, jailings and harassment. He was making final arrangements to move North on the day he was killed.*

1964: Jacksonville, Florida: **Johnnie Mae Chappell** *who cleaned houses to help support her family, was shot by four white men as she searched for a lost wallet along a roadside. The murder occurred during an outbreak of racial violence in downtown Jacksonville.*

1964: Cleveland, Ohio: **Rev. Bruce Klunder** *was among civil rights activists who protested the building of a segregated school by placing their bodies in the way of* *construction equipment. Klunder was crushed to death when a bulldozer backed over him.*

1964: Meadville, Mississippi: **Henry Hezekiah Dee and Charles Eddie Moore** *were killed by Klansmen who believed the two were part of a plot to arm blacks in the area (The Second Amendment did not apply to Blacks?). There was no such plot. Their bodies were found during a massive search for the missing civil rights workers Chaney, Goodman and Schwerner.*

1964: Philadelphia, Mississippi: **James Earl Chaney, Andrew Goodman, and Michael Henry Schwerner,** *young civil rights workers, were arrested by a deputy sheriff and then released into the hands of Klansmen who had plotted their murders. They were shot and their bodies buried in an earthen dam.*

1964: Colbert, Georgia: **Lt. Col. Lemuel Penn,** *a decorated World War II veteran, a Washington, D.C., educator, was driving home from U. S. Army Reserves training when he was shot and killed by Klansmen from a passing car.*

1965: Marion, Alabama: **Jimmie Lee Jackson** *was beaten and shot by state troopers as he tried to protect his grandfather and mother from a trooper attack on civil rights marchers. His death led to the Selma-Montgomery march and the eventual passage of the 1965 Voting Rights Act.*

1965: Selma, Alabama: **Rev. James Reeb,** *a Unitarian minister from Boston, was among many white clergymen who joined the Selma marchers after the attack by state troopers at the Edmund Pettus Bridge. Reeb was beaten to death by white men while he walked down a Selma street.*

1965: Selma Highway, Alabama: **Viola Gregg Liuzzo,** *a housewife and mother from Detroit, drove alone to Alabama to help with the Selma march after seeing televised reports of the attack at the Edmund Pettus Bridge. She was driving marchers back to Selma from Montgomery when she was shot and killed by a Klansman in a passing car. Mrs. Liuzzo was the first white woman killed during the Civil Rights struggles.*

1965: Bogalusa, Louisiana: **Oneal Moore** *was one of two black deputies hired by white officials in an attempt to appease civil rights demands. Moore and his partner Creed Rogers were on patrol when they were blasted with gunfire from a passing car. Moore was killed and Rogers was wounded.*

1965: Anniston, Alabama: **Willie Brewster** *was on his way home from work when he was shot and killed by white men. The men belonged to the National States Rights Party, a violent neo-Nazi group whose members had been involved in church bombings and murders of blacks.*

1965: Hayneville, Alabama: **Jonathan Myrick Daniels,** *an Episcopal Seminary student in Boston, had come to Alabama to help with black voter registration in Lowndes County. He was arrested at a demonstration, jailed in Hayneville and then suddenly released. Moments after his release, he was shot to death by a deputy sheriff.*

1966: Tuskegee, Alabama: **Samuel Leamon Younge, Jr.,** *a student civil rights activist, was fatally shot by a white gas station owner following an argument over segregated rest rooms.*

1966: Hattiesburg, Mississippi: **Vernon Ferdinand Dahmer,** *a wealthy businessman, offered to pay poll taxes for those who couldn't afford the fee required to vote. The night after a radio station broadcasted Dahmer's offer, his home was firebombed. Dahmer died later from severe burns.*

1966: Natchez, Mississippi: **Ben Chester White,** *who had worked most of his life as a caretaker on a plantation, had no involvement in civil rights work. He was murdered by Klansmen who thought they could divert attention from a civil rights march by killing a black person.*

1966: Bogalusa, Louisiana: **Clarence Triggs** *was a bricklayer who had attended civil rights meetings sponsored by the Congress of Racial Equality (CORE). He was found dead on a roadside, shot through the head.*

1967: Natchez, Mississippi: **Wharlest Jackson,** *the treasurer of his local NAACP chapter, was one of many blacks who had received threatening Klan notices at his job. After Jackson was promoted to a position previously reserved for whites, a bomb was planted in his car. It exploded minutes after he left work one day, killing him instantly.*

1967: Jackson, Mississippi: **Benjamin Brown,** *a former civil rights organizer, was watching a student protest from the sidelines when he was hit by stray gunshots from police who fired into the crowd.*

1968 Orangeburg, South Carolina: **Samuel Ephesians Hammond Jr., Delano Herman Middleton and Henry Ezekial Smith** *were shot and killed by police who fired on student demonstrators at the South Carolina State College campus.*

April 4, 1968: Memphis, Tennessee: **Dr. Martin Luther King, Jr.** *(No further explanation necessary)*

History will remember most of the names martyred during the Civil Rights era, especially, Medgar Evers and Dr. Martin Luther King, Jr., but it was the murder of 14 year old Emmitt Till that was the spark that lit the firestorm that became the Civil Rights movement.

24

The Greatest Generation And Fair Housing

The history of housing for black Americans parallels the history of blacks in the military, black enfranchisement, black education and black employment. It was a struggle, is a struggle, and will continue to be a struggle. To paraphrase William Faulkner, "The past is not dead, in fact it isn't even past."

In states where there were no laws requiring segregation, separation among the races still occurred because of residential housing patterns. Such patterns were not accidental, but were simply the result of free market selection on the part of home buyers. Housing patterns were the orchestrated result of housing ordinances, and the racial steering of real estate brokers, the lending practices of bankers, and the collective action of white homeowners.[97]

In my own experience, in 1974, we were relocated by the government as a result of a job promotion and looked for a home in Cerritos, California, a Southern California suburb. My wife and I entered a local real estate office and couldn't get the attention of an agent until I asserted myself and said, "We're looking to purchase a house in this area." The agent informed us that there were no homes for our kind in Cerritos, but we should look in other areas. I told him we had $20,000 cash money for a down payment, and he quickly jumped up and said, "Let me show you some properties!" We said no thanks and left.

Sometime after World War I, responding to the beginning migrations of blacks from the rural south, zoning laws were established, especially in the Mid Atlantic States, that forbade a "colored person" from moving into a neighborhood where a majority of white residents lived. As is their wont, blacks went to court and appealed zoning laws and were supported by the Supreme Court in a 1917 decision referred to as Buchanan v. Warley.

---

[97] Beverly Daniel Tatum, PHD. *"Can We Talk about Race"?* Beacon Press, Boston, MA pg. 3.

So did that solve the problem of discrimination in housing? No, because folks again used the interpretations of the law to mean that "government could not discriminate by zoning methods," but contracts between private individual did not apply; therefore, throughout the United States, Restrictive Covenant agreements were established to prevent blacks to rent or buy property as per their wishes.

Restrictive Covenants were inserted into deeds and became conditions of buying and selling property privately, and they were enforced by the agents of the buyers and sellers, Real Estate Boards and Home Owner Associations.

"The practice was so widespread that by 1940, 80 percent of property in Chicago and Los Angeles carried restrictive covenants barring black families." [98]

Any free market advocate would understand what happens when supply is manipulated, prices go up and as a result, the market of housing for blacks, limited to only certain parts of a community were artificially raised.

One of the innovative enterprises that arose after World War II was the community of Levittown. The GI Bill of Rights included housing provisions and the folks who built Levittown, capitalized on this factor. A returning veteran could purchase a home complete with appliances, landscaping, a fireplace, vertical blinds for $7,990, without making a down payment.

The families who were becoming home owners and establishing equity were mostly blue collar workers, heavily unionized with full medical benefits, and most worked in the new "military-industrial" businesses. Residents formed Rotary clubs, were on school boards and were influential in political clubs.

Levittown was the American Dream. However, Levittown had a dark secret—it was racially exclusive. African Americans were denied access to this American dream. Every deed signed by new home owners contained a clause that bound them "not to permit the premises to be used or occupied by any other person than members of the Caucasian race."

I have been recently made aware of such a restrictive covenant in the will of a well known pioneer of one of our more local affluent communities, and frankly, I was shocked as the person has schools, parks and libraries named after her. The California I grew up in never made bigotry a disqualifier.

---

[98] "Understanding Fair Housing." U.S. Commission on Civil Rights Clearinghouse Publication 42, Feburary 1973. Retrieved 8/4/2011

It was not an accident that black folks just happened to live in the "lower parts of New Orleans" and white folk lived on the high ground. A century of restrictive covenants made it so, and as a result, black folks lost their homes, white folk did not.

I think we have discussed the history of segregation long enough to understand that various methods were used to keep the races apart, and in many cases, the methods, practices, etc. were endorsed by the Courts. From the beginning, making Blacks three-fifths of a person for determining a state's population to the "40 Acres and a Mule," blacks have attempted to be property owners and were denied equal access to the law and the land.

We have seen prior to the Civil War, the courts refusing to recognize any rights for black persons, whether they were slaves or free. The federal government did very little to prohibit discrimination, and even those states that had abolished slavery treated blacks as inferior.

The ideology of the time is well illustrated in the 1857 Dred Scott case where the Court held that persons of African descent were not citizens of the United States entitled to any rights. According to the Court, the black man had no rights the white man was bound to respect. The Court stated that this principle applied to all black persons, slave or free.

In my opinion, in the final analysis, the Civil War was about human dignity and human rights, however, there were many who did not get the memo and the struggle went on.

The Civil Rights Act of 1866 guaranteed property rights to all citizens regardless of race. Every American had the same rights to inherit, purchase, and sell real and personal property.

But there has always been a caveat in our methods. Things are never as simple as they appear. Remember the Supreme Court cases where the courts explained that the Constitution only applied to acts of government and not of individuals? This is where they got around state enforcement of "the people's rights to own property." You could buy private property only if someone wanted to sell it to you. There was no inherent right for anyone to buy any property, said the courts, unless someone was willing to sell it to you.

And as long as the state was not involved, all property deals were private and restrictive covenants were legal; however, along comes another interesting Supreme Court case.

A black family by the name of Shelley bought a home in St. Louis, Missouri and before they moved in, a neighbor named Louis Kraemer, who lived 10 blocks away, sued Shelley and prevented the Shelley family from moving into their new home.

The Supreme Court of Missouri, the "Dredful" Dred Scott State, ruled in favor of Kraemer and therefore, exercising their rights, Shelley took the case to the U.S. Supreme Court in 1948, where they were represented by Thurgood Marshall and Loren Miller.

The Supreme Court held up the rights of Kraemer and the rights of private citizens to control the buyer-purchase activity, even though it appeared to be discriminatory. However, the Court stipulated, the enforcement of the restrictive covenants *could not* be accomplished through any state action. They said that any state action, enforcing the restrictive covenants laws, would violate the equal protection clause of the Fourteenth Amendment.

A little complicated? Briefly, folks had the right to discriminate in the selling of property, but the courts could not enforce those rights. Enforcement had to come some other way.

Attorneys Marshall and Miller would gain fame as the attorneys for Brown in the landmark Brown v. Board of Education case, reversing the "separate but equal" decision in Plessy. The Brown case outlawed segregation in schools and marked the beginning of the end of the era of legalized segregation.

Despite the efforts of Presidents Kennedy and Johnson, various Executive Orders and amendments to Civil Rights Laws did not do much to improve the housing market for black people and other minorities. Both the executive orders and changes to the Civil Rights law had to do with housing provided by the Government, or housing financed by the Government. It still did not infringe upon the rights of private individuals to determine how to sell their homes.

In 1968, Congress passed a law banning discrimination on the basis of race, color, religion, and national origin in public or private transactions. Second, the U.S. Supreme Court resurrected the Civil Rights Act of 1866 and used it to fight racial discrimination. The landmark case was Jones v. Alfred H. Mayer Co., where the Warren court ruled that the state could regulate the sale of private property in order to prevent racial discrimination and enforce the intent of the Thirteenth Amendment.

This was another moment that the Warren Court over ruled the Taney Court and another example that we are a nation of laws, interpreted by man, given their biases and times in which they live. In April 1968, Martin Luther King was assassinated, just prior to the signing of the anti-discrimination laws which set the mood favorably to the sponsors of the bill.

Over time, Congress and Presidents have strengthened the Fair Housing Laws that also included Fair Lending laws in public or private transactions, including enacting penalties to those who fail to comply with the laws. The new laws also included the prohibition of gender discrimination, which was important to families where women were the sole providers.

President Ronald Reagan signed the Fair Housing Amendments Act of 1988. The Amendment expanded the coverage of the Fair Housing Act and made major changes to the law, including adding two protected classes to the Fair Housing Act: (1) families with children and (2) handicapped persons. The Amendment also strengthened the government's ability to enforce the Fair Housing Act and removed the cap on punitive damages and increased the available damages and civil penalties.

It has been reported that home ownership represents almost 70 percent of the wealth owned by black Americans compared with 38 percent of wealth tied up in home ownership by white Americans. The 2000 through 2006 subprime loan practices, where Blacks refinanced at a greater rate than whites, wiped out billions of dollars of black wealth, wealth that will take generations to recover. Wealth that was once owned by black Americans is now owned by financial institutions.

So blacks have taken a step backwards, at a time when home ownership is the single most important stabilizer to home life, to security and the first practical evidence in owning part of the American dream. Can blacks bounce back quickly? Only time will tell, but if history is prologue, it will take a long, long time, unless we have some breakthrough solutions.

25

Kerner Report

1968. This was the year that Martin Luther King and Bobby Kennedy were assassinated, and America saw another year of volatile race riots on television. They were called race riots, but really, they weren't. They were protest riots in black communities. Blacks did not rush the white communities and destroy them—they stayed in their own communities and destroyed their own homes, streets, and businesses, many which were owned by non-whites and corporations. Can you have a race riot if only one race is involved?

Is suicide a murder? Probably legally it is, but they call it suicide. What should we call it when communities commit suicide?

The government, under President Johnson, published a "white paper" describing the causes of the riots of 1968. It was subsequently referred to as the Kerner Report, named after its chairman, Otto Kerner, Governor of Illinois. The report caused a political stir in the United States from both the left and the right of our political cultures. The timing made it difficult as it was published in March 1968, and Martin Luther King was assassinated in April 1968, followed by Bobby Kennedy's assassination in June, 1968.

The nation's emotions were already strained with Vietnam at its peak. The Commission studied the causes of the riots of 1968, and while saying that a growing black militancy may have added fuel to the riots, they rejected the idea that there had been any organization behind the outbreaks. Instead, the Commission blamed the violence on the devastating poverty and endemic of hopelessness in the inner cities of the 1960s.

Among their many findings:

- One in five African-Americans lived in squalor and deprivation in ghetto neighborhoods.

- The unemployment rate was double for African-Americans, as compared to whites.

- Communities were neglected by their government, wracked with crime, and traumatized by police brutality.

- Disproportionate rates of infant mortality were astounding—African-American children were dying at triple the rate of white children.

The information was not surprising or new. But the Kerner Commission went further than normally a government panel will; that is, they assigned blame for the conditions of black America. The Kerner Commission placed the blame for the plight of black America on white racism. The report stated, "what white Americans have never fully understood—but what the Negro can never forget—is that the white society is deeply implicated in the ghetto. White institutions created it. White institutions maintain it, and white society condones it."

The report's conclusion and it's most memorable message was this—"our nation is moving towards two societies, one white, one black, separate and unequal."[99]

The liberal left embraced the findings, while the conservative right condemned the reasoning and findings. Subsequently, America drifted further apart in addressing the issues of black America and failed to settle on a permanent solution, if there ever was one. But it is undeniable, America had failed its black citizens, and in fact, the inability to even acknowledge the "sins committed over time" prevented a reasonable solution.

The debate continued. Forty years after the Kerner Report was published and years after liberal solutions to the problems failed to permanently reduce poverty, inequality, racial injustice and crime another report was published by the *Eisenhower Foundation* in February 2008.

What has happened in the last 40 years?

Poverty:

- African Americans are three times as likely as non-Hispanic Whites to live in deep poverty, below half the poverty line.

---

[99] [Kerner Commission Report Forty Years After. Eisenhower Foundation Updates, Interview by Bill Moyers of Fred Harris, former U.S, Senator, Oklahoma and member of Kerner Commission]

- Unemployment and underemployment were the most important causes of poverty, yet African American unemployment has continued to be twice as high as White unemployment during each of the last four decades.

- Among high school drop outs, aged 19, only 38 percent of African Americans are employed, compared to 67 percent of Whites.

Inequality: Income and Wealth:

- The top one percent of the population (300,000 Americans) now receives as much income as the lower half of the population (150 million Americans).

- Since the late 1970s, the real after tax income of those at the top of the income scale has grown 200 percent, while it has grown by 15 percent for those in the middle and 9 percent for those at the bottom.

- A recent Brookings Institution study on mobility found that 68 percent of white children from middle income families grew up to surpass their parents income in real terms, but that share was only 31 percent for middle income African American children.

- In terms of wealth, America is the most unequal country in the industrialized world.

Inequality-Wages:

- Over the last 40 years, America has had the most rapid growth in wage inequality in the industrial world.

- Since the 1970s, productivity has increased significantly in America, but wages have increased little in real terms. From November 2001 through July 2006, worker wages grew at an annual rate of 1.6 percent, while profits grew at an annual rate of 14.4 percent.

- In the 1960s, the average CEO earned about 40 times more than the average worker. Today, the average CEO earns about 360 times as much.

- Among full time workers, whites earn over 22 percent more than equivalent African American workers.

Inequality-Education:

- Large disparities remain in America between the educational achievement of White and Asian American high school students compared to Latino and Black high school students.

- American educational disparities remain linked to funding disparities. The wealthiest ten percent of school districts in the U.S. spend nearly ten times more than the poorest ten percent.

- In the U.S., the highest performing students from low income families now enroll in college at the same rate as the lowest performing students from high income families. In other words, the smartest poor kids attend college at the same rate as the dumbest rich kids.

Racial Injustice:

- The likelihood for the death penalty is greater for blacks than whites. Blacks receive longer sentences than whites for the same crimes. Sentences for crack cocaine, used disproportionately by minorities, have been much longer than sentences for powder cocaine, used disproportionately by whites.

- There is continuing evidence from distinguished scholars that some employers "steer" minority applicants into the worst jobs regardless of their qualifications; that many real estate agents steer minorities to less desirable locations, compared to whites; and that lenders treat minorities differently from whites in terms of percentage of mortgage applications accepted.

Crime:

- There has been an eight fold increase in the total population of persons in prisons and jails since the late 1960s. Well over 2,000,000 persons now are in American prisons and jails. America has the highest reported rate of incarceration in the world.

- African American men aged 25 to 29 are almost seven times as likely to be incarcerated as their white counterparts.

- Today, the rate of incarceration of African American men in the U.S. is four times higher than the rate of incarceration of black South Africans in South Africa during the pre-Nelson Mandela apartheid government.

- A prison—industrial complex has developed. The states collectively now spend more on prison construction than on construction for higher education.

American liberals used the report to justify numerous government programs such as the continuation of the War on Poverty, Affirmative Action and other Civil Rights legislation. The conservative movement in our country has felt that most of the liberal policies were failures. Both are right and both are wrong. The need for a solution to the gross level of poverty, discrimination in all areas of American life continues.

There is a shared value amongst liberals and conservatives, an American value, that I call the Value of Fairness. Americans want their systems and processes to be fair and competitive and when things appear unfair, America will root for the underdog. Both progressives and conservatives want a fair deal in competition in sports or business. Either side finds a stacked deck offensive. Liberals feel that African Americans have not had a fair deal and Conservatives agree in part, but they feel the deal is fair now and using Affirmative Action methods to advance blacks, or anyone, is wrong, because it is unfair to others.

The majority feel that giving a member of a minority a "free ride" is unfair and the minorities feel the same way when members of the majority get "free rides" into colleges or into corporate positions. In fact, many minorities believe that when "Affirmative Action was White," the majority was given an insurmountable advantage economically, socially and politically. However, nothing lowers morale in an enterprise more than when there is a perception that personnel systems are unfair. When perception is reality, the appearance of unfairness is devastating to an institution or enterprise.

I do not feel this will ever change because absurdly, both are correct. The value of fairness is unique in American culture and it should be preserved. Although there are many myths about Affirmative Action, some of which I will discuss, Affirmative Action benefiting minorities, especially blacks, appears unfair to white males and will always be resisted; therefore, I shall not recommend it as a solution, in its present form.

A personal experience from my executive days in the Postal Service sheds light on white paranoia on Affirmative Action. It was not uncommon that whenever I promoted a minority, especially a Hispanic person, into a position of prominence, we would receive anonymous letters about the evils of Affirmative Action and predictions that things were going to get worse as the new executive was going to promote Mexicans, regardless of more qualified whites being available.

There were always qualified whites available in a talent pool; however, notwithstanding their paradigm, they were not always the "best qualified."

I once played in a charity golf tournament and was introduced on the first tee as, "the Postmaster of Sacramento." A member of the audience said, loud enough for me and others to hear, "they always give minorities those jobs!" The truth was that I was the first minority to ever be promoted to the Postmaster's job in Sacramento after 150 years of white male Postmasters. Hardly a trend! A peculiar thing about minorities is we have sensitive ears. My high school coach called this phenomenon, having "rabbit ears."

The purpose of Affirmative Action government sponsored programs was to overcome previous injustices that had given one segment of our population an advantage in employment and education. Historically, white males have been given preference in entrance to colleges and universities, in employment and upward mobility and in the availability of certain trades and professions.

The preference of white males over the decades has given minorities and females a distinct disadvantage as they entered the market place, attempting to compete against the entrenched system.

I enjoyed working in an industry that employed thousands of minorities and females, and have first-hand knowledge about Affirmative Action programs in the public sector. I have also interacted with fellow professionals in the Personnel profession who worked in the private sector. The issues of Equal Employment Opportunity were similar in the public and private sector.

It was my experience that much of Equal Employment Opportunity programs, and specifically Affirmative Action were misunderstood and consciously resisted by those in charge of implementing policy. Similar to the Admirals and Generals who failed to execute policy promptly and smartly after President Truman ordered the desegregation of the Armed Forces, many executives in the Postal Service also dragged their feet in implementing the "spirit and intent" of the civil rights laws.

I was privileged to introduce three national policy programs to executives of the Postal Service. One as regional manager of Equal Employment Opportunity programs, with the responsibility of assisting Postal executives in drafting EEO Affirmative Action plans, which included targets and timetables. Two, I was a member of a national steering committee introducing Participative Management to the Postal Service, wherein management and craft employees worked together to improve the quality of work life of all employees and thereby, improving the effectiveness of the enterprise and Three, I was a Regional Manager of the Total Quality Management program in the Postal Service.

Each of the programs were resisted from the onset for three reasons—(1) Executives felt that they already were practicing equal employment opportunity for all employees, (2) Executives felt they were already participating with employees in the business of the enterprise and (3) Quality management was their forte.

So why change? Why did they resist? Affirmative action programs were designed to change the existing paradigm and challenged existing hiring and promotion systems, that for the most part, favored the "look-a-likes" of the executives we were trying to change. It was no surprise that they resisted, and was certainly understandable.

There was less resistance when we implemented the Affirmative Action program for women, as many of the inheritors were "look-a-likes" of their mothers, sisters, daughters, and wives.

Over time, a cottage industry of myths of Affirmative Action has been developed and I will address them from my own bank of experience.

Myths about Affirmative Action:

Myth 1. *The only way to create a color-blind society is to adopt color-blind policies.*

Sounds good! Unfortunately, a color blind policy, set in a country that over the centuries did not use color blind personnel systems, to now adopt it would ignore past discriminatory practices. Seniority systems used to promote or demote inversely, always favored the white employee as he was the first hired and minorities were the last hired. Likewise, color-blind college admissions favored white students because of their earlier educational advantages, and a system of legacy admissions. Unless preexisting inequities are identified and corrected, color-blind policies do not correct racial injustice. Unless an outside influence is introduced, outcomes will remain the same as before.

Myth 2. *Affirmative Action has not succeeded in increasing female and minority representation.*

Wrong! Affirmative Action programs have been successful, in spite of some foot dragging. The purpose of Affirmative Action was to increase the number of minorities and women in employment and to increase the same in higher level positions. The Department of Labor documented over 5 million minority members and 6 million white and minority women that have moved up in the workforce, directly as a result of Affirmative Action programs. Contractors doing business with the government, who were required to develop Affirmative Action plans added black and female officials and managers at twice the rate of contractors not doing business with the government.

There have also been a number of large private companies, multi-nationals, increasing minority employment as a result of adopting affirmative action policies.

Myth 3. *The public did not support affirmative action.*

Public opinion polls said otherwise. What the general public never liked was a quota system. Quota systems, they believed, would permit the probability of promoting "lesser qualified candidates" in order to reach an artificial target. The majority of Americans supported affirmative action, and especially thought it was a good idea to open our employment markets to all segments of society. The public was convinced that "fair employment policies" were the best way to manage an enterprise.

Myth 4. *A large percentage of White workers will lose out if affirmative action is continued.*

It was never true that Affirmative Action had a measurable negative output against white males. The numbers just do not add up, and similar to the story that "the Postal Service always *gives* jobs to people like that," it is a myth perpetuated by folks who have seen their paradigm challenged.

Look at the data without passion. There were 1.3 million unemployed Black civilians and 112 million employed White civilians in 2000 according to the U.S. Bureau of the Census. If every unemployed black worker in the United States were to displace a white worker, only 1% of Whites would be affected. The main sources of job loss among white workers have to do with factory relocations and lower labor costs outside the United States, computerization and automation, and corporate downsizing.

In the most recent years, jobs have been lost as a result of the loss of demand for goods and services in the United States and the increase of the same in South America and Europe. American companies are increasing their investments to where the sales are growing.

Unfortunately, cases of "reverse discrimination" get more press than regular incidents of discrimination. The cases are similar to "white woman abducted" cases. It completely distorts that discrimination exists in all segments of our society, and more often against black applicants. You just don't read about it in the paper.

Myth 5. *If Immigrants from Europe can rapidly advance economically, African Americans should be able to do the same.*

This can only be believed if the reader has not read the previous chapters of my book. Blacks have a 500 year history on this continent: Almost 250 years involving slavery, 100 more years involving legalized discrimination and then the subtle years of shunning and passiveness by America. The European immigrants arriving in America included doctors, lawyers, professors and entrepreneurs among their ranks, and they had a shared history and were white, and quickly assimilated into the American fabric through inter-marriage and acceptance of American values and culture.

An interesting history of immigration and assimilation can be found in the history of the Knights of Columbus, the Catholic Church's largest social and benevolent order. Founded in the 1880s, it assisted the new Irish and Italian immigrants almost from the time the new immigrant would get off the boat and helped them to find jobs, homes and "catholic schools" throughout the Eastern seaboard, which the new immigrants attended.

The Knights of Columbus did not accept blacks into their organization until 1950.

Myth 6. *Affirmative action tends to undermine the self-esteem of women and racial minorities.*

Nothing could be further from the truth. In my experience working with thousands of black and minority folks, I never once found one whose self-esteem was an issue as a result of them getting a job or getting promoted. Not once!

There is nothing so debilitating to the human condition as unemployment. "Unemployment always wounds the victim's dignity and threatens the equilibrium of his life. Besides the harm done to him personally, it entails numerous risks for his family."[100]

What could possibly be worse than not working? If minorities felt that they did not deserve the job that they were "given," it is news to me and totally not my experience. If this be the case, white men, who have traditionally benefited from preferential employment, certainly did not feel hampered by self-doubt or a loss in self-esteem.

What you feel after years of preferential treatment is entitlement!

---

[100] Catechism of the Catholic Church. Second Edition, LIBRERIA EDITRICE VATICANA. Section 2436

My experience was that affirmative action actually raised the self-esteem of women and minorities by providing them with employment and opportunities for advancement. I am betting on this in my solution to our problem. Believe me, the unemployed suffer more from lack of self-esteem than folks who are employed and folks who gain through affirmative action programs usually have greater job satisfaction and are more committed to company effectiveness.

Myth 7. *Affirmative action is nothing more than an attempt at social engineering by liberal Democrats.*

Totally not true. Affirmative Action, might be an attempt at social engineering, as were previous hiring and firing programs have been; however, government sponsored Affirmative Action programs which began under President John F. Kennedy received support from Republican presidents as well as Democrat presidents. Richard Nixon did as much as any Democrat President and encouraged Affirmative Action in the government advancing civil rights. Under Mr. Nixon, the government introduced the Hispanic Affirmative Action programs in 1972 and signed a myriad of bills designed to promote minority business in government contracting. Nixon, more than most presidents, expanded the government's ability to enforce the 1965 Voting Rights Act.

Ronald Reagan was the most contrarian of Presidents with respect to Affirmative Action as he postulated against any government efforts to intercede with the private and public sectors in employment and private personnel policies. He attempted to repeal Affirmative Action executive orders, but was unsuccessful. Mr. Reagan did sign a bill improving the ability of Minority Business Enterprises to compete for government grants and contracts.

Myth 8. *Support for affirmative action means support for preferential selection-procedures that favor unqualified candidates over qualified candidates.*

Nothing disrupts an enterprise more than to promote unqualified people to jobs they cannot perform superbly. Supporters of affirmative action oppose this type of preferential selection. It is unfortunate that unqualified people sometimes did get assigned to positions for which they were not prepared, and this happened with respect to the white majority as well as to the minority candidate. The issue of fairness is strong in the American culture and obvious evidence of less qualified folks receiving positions, where other more qualified candidates are bypassed, quickly surfaces in business communities. They are almost always looked upon with disgust.

Unfortunately, when white men were promoted to positions when they were not as qualified as others, society appeared to accept that as "business as usual" and learned to live with it, but over time, this also wilted confidence in the selection processes.

There will be some who will say that we have come a long way, and they would be right. Affirmative Action activities of the latter 20th Century certainly improved the lot of many minorities, women and blacks, but Affirmative Action is a now a dead strategy. Affirmative Action, like Reparations or Amnesty are "fighting words," that inflame main street America and has no champion in the political arena and cannot be depended upon to solve our age old problem.

Over time, Management introduced concepts in industry to improve business; Total Quality Management (TQM) being one of them. Total Quality Management operates on a principle of continuous improvement of processes to improve a product or service. Every part of the business practices TQM to eliminate waste, redundancy and capture costs. Continuous improvement is incremental and goes on to infinity and continuously improves the enterprise.

Let me give you an elementary look at Total Quality Management (TQM), so we can better understand Affirmative Action.

The hypothetical problem we are trying to fix: *Getting to work on time.* Apparently you have been late often enough that you have to question the "processes" that get you to work, and make them work better to your favor.

The Process: The steps of the process are identified, so we can examine those events that cause us the biggest problem: Alarm goes off at 0600. You crawl out of bed at 0601. You take a bathroom break, including shower and a shave completed by 0620. Dress, prepare and eat breakfast, leave the house by 0645. Travel fifteen miles and arrive at work no later than 0715 on twenty occasions over the last thirty days. Official time to begin work is 0730 each day, so you are late one-third of the time—totally unacceptable!

The good news is that you are never late more than five minutes.

From the moment that the alarm rings to the moment you arrive at your work site and clock in represent one giant process. In order to always get to work on time, you examine every portion of the process, until you find the solution.

A process will remain constant and does not vary measurably unless something different is introduced. The improvement of the process can be subtle or significant. A subtle improvement is usually referred to as an incremental improvement and a significant improvement is a "breakthrough" improvement.

The problem of getting to work on time can be more complex than I described as more factors could be involved, such as, maybe there is a husband that has to be fed, or children that have to be fed, clothed and sent off to school. Nevertheless, getting to work on time is your responsibility and you have to solve the problem and to do so, we look into the process. This is, in business, called Process Management.

When we identify the components of the process, and tweak them subtlety, and improve our chances of getting to work on time, and we do it consistently, we have made a continuous improvement.

A breakthrough improvement is not so subtle. In order to assure that we will always get to work on time, we sell our home and rent an apartment next to the place we work. That is a not so subtle way to improve the process as you eliminated the entire time you spent on the road to get to work. The impact of the "breakthrough strategy" is monumental and impacts the lives of your family, and possibly many other families.

In business, TQM is introduced to incrementally improve the enterprise continuously. Every day, in every way, the business improves its output or service. Every once in a while the business has to improve its performance quicker. It might be that they have priced itself above their competitor or it might be they are not getting their product to their customer as fast as their competitor; whatever, they need something other than a subtle improvement.

They need breakthrough performance. Normally "breakthrough" performance that is sustaining requires the introduction of new capital or new ideas and the challenging of existing paradigms. It may also need the retraining of the workforce for the sudden change, while continuous improvement is introduced into the work force incrementally and accepted as natural. Breakthrough performance savings are almost immediate while a continuous improvement process may take months or years to capture similar savings.

Affirmative Action, introduced as a result of the Civil Rights legislation of the 1960's, was the breakthrough performance needed for black Americans to break down barriers to employment, promotions, housing and education.

Breakthrough performance in business does not come without some pain to the status quo; oftentimes layoffs and redistribution of labor is the result. Affirmative Action in America had considerable pain to the status quo, requiring the bypassing of folks whose expectations were not realized as others, normally not in competition for the same jobs in earlier times, now were promoted to the new positions.

America has had little problem in rationalizing the discrimination of blacks during the Jim Crow era and turned their eyes in the period after, and would have done very little to improve the lot of Black Americans without the Revolution called the "Civil Rights movement." However, discriminating against whites, "reverse discrimination" is treated as Un-American, in the minds of folks in power. After all did not Martin Luther King, Jr., say that folks "should be judged by the nature of their character and not by the color of their skins?"

Affirmative Action is dead and served its purpose and we do not intend to mourn her nor resurrect her; however, we still need another form of "breakthrough performance." However, this breakthrough performance will not be painful to anyone; there will be no layoffs, nor denial of promotions nor any preferential treatment for anyone. It will be in the full tradition of our American culture; that is, folks will be rewarded for their hard work, ingenuity, and enterprise. But there will be a required investment by our government, both federal and state, to finance the process. Don't worry, we will get our money back ten-fold.

How should America atone for her sins? It is my judgment that Black Americans have been victims of a government conspiracy, both de jure and de facto, both with eyes wide open and eyes wide shut, and they conspired with fellow citizens. I also believe that the situation has improved over time and there has been incremental improvement; however, it is too little and too late to offset the trends of putting more blacks in prison and preventing blacks from realizing a competitive status in the challenges facing all Americans.

I know that many folks will point out that many blacks have succeeded like Colin Powell, Condoleeza Rice, Oprah Winfrey, Barack Obama and others. But again I ask, how many black school teachers do you know? How many Engineers, Pharmacists, Doctors, Lawyers, Plumbers, High School Principals, Dentists, City Managers, Scientists, Draftsmen, Architects, Stock Brokers, Paralegals, College Presidents, Professors and owners of small businesses do you know who are black?

In every generation, blacks have prospered in spite of the obstacles. I have attempted to outline the lives of a few of them throughout this work, from colonial periods through the Civil War and Reconstruction Periods, through the Gilded Age and the early 20th Century through the present; however, each generation also perpetuated and reinforced the *unworthiness* of blacks to participate fully in American society.

In my friend Harold's lifetime, he was born seventy-three years after the signing of the 13th Amendment which emancipated the slaves, he witnessed the first black to play Major League baseball in 1947, the first black to play on the PGA Golf tour in

1961, not because they were never good enough, but because "the rules" prevented them from participating. He witnessed the first black mayors of large American cities, the first black U.S. Senator since Reconstruction, the first black General, and the first black Admiral and the first black President.

Harold attended segregated schools in the mid 1950s and attended Memphis State University where blacks could not join Fraternities, could not live in on-campus dormitories, and could not fraternize with white co-eds. In the "New South," where he grew up, a college education for a black man promised you a teacher's job in a black public school, or maybe, if lucky, a job as a letter carrier in large city Post Offices. The letter carrier job was open to blacks in the "New South," but positions in the office staff, clerks and administration jobs, were not available to blacks in the Post Office. Positions serving the public directly, face to face, were not available to black employees.

Initial level supervisory positions were given to Postal employees who passed a Civil Service examination slanted to knowledge gained primarily in the clerk craft.

Harold met the first black Postmaster of Los Angeles; however, he has never experienced the appointment of a black Postmaster General.

Harold remembers his grandfather who was lynched by whites, who got away with it. He remembers Jim Crow as if it was yesterday and remains suspicious of white generosity or white motives. Affirmative Action was a gift reluctantly accepted. Blacks were not ungrateful, just suspicious. Affirmative Action gave many blacks opportunities that would not have been available in normal circumstances and the facts indicate that economic gains were made as a result. The Brookings Institution found economic gains lifted entire black populations into the middle class following the civil-rights movement and Affirmative Actions. However, those gains, the Institution claims, have actually reversed for their children. The study said, "a majority of blacks born to middle-income parents grow up to have less income than their parents."

I remember my father, a truly fair man, mentioning to us that "blacks will advance someday, but they are asking for too much, too fast. They should bide their time!" Even the best intentioned folks in our society played a role in holding back blacks over the years.

"Only 31 percent of black children born to parents in the middle of the income distribution have family income greater than their parents, compared to 68 percent of white children from the same income bracket, "the Brookings Institute study noted. "White children are more likely to move up the ladder while black children are more likely to fall down."[101]

The end result of centuries old prejudice and bigotry woven into the American fabric is that blacks inhabit the lower echelons of American society. Certainly many will point out the successes of Blacks in sports, entertainment and in some instances, in business. This only proves my theory that given an equal playing field, blacks will succeed as well as any other group.

Unfortunately, we have not prepared blacks to succeed in the normal everyday playing field of commerce. The American government, both Federal and State, have conspired and collaborated with white society, to hold back black people, people of color, Negroes, Creoles, and African-Americans by legal and illegal means. Blacks have not had the same opportunities as the rest of society to create wealth by accumulating real property, by not being provided equal and quality education, and by preventing them from acquiring the full joy of patriotism in the Armed Forces, and denying them the full potential benefits of the G.I Bill of Rights, and by continuing to ignore the plight of contemporary blacks.

Now that blacks are welcome in the military, the G.I Bill of Rights has diminished in value as it no longer pays for a full college education. I am not claiming that it has lost its purchasing power because blacks are potential beneficiaries, but the fact is that blacks are not benefiting as whites did after World II and the Korean conflict, where the G.I Bill paid in full a complete five year college education.

Contemporary American blacks are the beneficiaries of the American black and white history. It is time to correct the ship of state. It is time to atone for America's Original Sin and I feel there is a solution that puts the burden where it belongs and where it will be welcomed.

---

[101] Lewis Diuguid, Riverside Press Enterprise, January 21, 2008

26

The Solution

Did the Founding Fathers have a solution to America's Black/White dilemma?

In a letter written by Edward Coles in 1814 to Thomas Jefferson, he implored:

> *"My object is to entreat and beseech you to exert your knowledge and influence in devising and getting into operation some plan for the gradual emancipation of slavery.... In the calm of your retirement you might, most beneficially to society, and with much addition to your own fame . . . put into complete practice those hallowed principles contained in that renowned Declaration, of which you were the immortal author".*

Jefferson replied in a long letter, which can be summed up in the following:

> *"No, I have over lived the generation with mutual labors and perils begat mutual confidence and influence. This enterprise is for the young, for those who can follow it up and bear it through to consummation. It shall have all my prayers, and these are the only weapons of an old man."*[102]

Not all Founding Fathers rested after retirement from the Washington scene.

Benjamin Franklin, the old Founder, retired and became an elder statesman and in his last foray into public policy, he became president of the Pennsylvania Society for the Abolition of Slavery and was asked to develop a plan for the introduction of former slaves into American society.

---

[102] Blumrosen, Alfred W. & Blumrosen, Ruth G. *SLAVE NATION, How Slavery United the Colonies & Sparked the American Revolution.* Sourcebooks Inc. Naperville, Illinois. 2005. page 247

In 1789, on behalf of the society, he wrote the following policy statement with an accompanying plan:

> *"Slavery is such an atrocious debasement of human nature that its very extirpation, if not performed with solicitous care, may sometimes open a source of serious evils . . . To instruct, to advise, to qualify those who have been restored to freedom, for the exercise and enjoyment of civil liberties, to promote in them habits of industry, to furnish them with employment suited to their age, sex, talents, and other circumstances, and to procure their children an education calculated for their future situation in life, these are the great outlines of the annexed plan."*[103]

The plan had four components, each to be carried out by a committee of the Pennsylvania Society for the Abolition of Slavery. The first component was a committee to assist with advice, instructions, and protection from wrongs to the former slaves, concern for their morals and "other friendly services." The second was a committee of guardians to facilitate the training and education of children and young people. The third was a committee on education to influence the children to attend "the schools already established in this city, or form others with this view." The fourth was a committee of employ, who "shall endeavour to procure constant employment" for laborers and to help them become apprentices in the skilled trades and also "assist in commencing business, such as appears to be qualified for it."[104]

The time is now! Benjamin Franklin has waited long enough. America is better equipped culturally and philosophically to do the right thing now; that is, apologize to our black Americans and to assure their future and ours is brighter, with the same hope and aspirations that all Americans have at their birth in this great land and that all immigrants have when they come to these shores.

I am reminded of 1 Corinthians 13:13 . . ."So faith, hope, love remain, these three, but the greatest of these is love."

With love in my heart, I propose the following as the ONLY solution to our self-created problem.

BE IT ENACTED FOR 100 YEARS AFTER THE LEGISLATION BECOMES LAW.

Grades K through 12:

---

[103] Slave Nation, ibid. page 253
[104] Slave Nation, ibid. page 254

- In communities (neighborhoods) where the black population is the majority, a sufficient number of classrooms will be available so that no more than fifteen children will ever be in any one classroom.

- In communities (neighborhoods) where the black population is the majority, a sufficient number of police and security personnel will be available to guarantee the safety of the children from the home to the school and vice-versa, every day school is open.

- The special security force in black communities, which will be an integral part of the local police force, will be known as "Buffalo Soldiers" to remind one and all of the great tradition this organization played in protecting white settlers in the American west. The uniforms of this special force should be typical of the old west "Buffalo Soldiers."

- Every black person in America, who is otherwise eligible and qualified, will be entitled to full tuition, books and supplies, and a stipend for room and board, to attend any state funded university, college, or trade school in the United States. The stipend for room and board shall be equal to what athletes receive at a typical Division 1 University.

- The duration of the voucher for this education will be the equivalent of five years, whether semesters or quarters.

There will be no attempt at traditional Affirmative Action, no compromising of any school standard; however, the denial of enrollment to any State university or college will not be unreasonable and will be subject to review and appeal.

The definition of a "black person" will be the definition used by the majority opinion in Plessy v. Ferguson (i.e. one-eighth African blood).

The "College Voucher" program will be available to the heirs of black slaves and other "colored" victims of segregation. An assumption will be made that any black person currently living in this country whose ancestry goes back at least to the early part of the 20th Century, is descended from slavery and oppressed by the Jim Crow laws of the 19th and 20th Centuries.

Some folks will say that reparations to blacks are too expensive, and I say to them, that it is not. It has already been paid for by black Americans and we who have not suffered their fate are in debt to them.

Now is the time to pay our debts.

Benefits to society:

We will be able to see, almost immediately, the rise of hope and the lowering of despair and the rise of expectations in our black communities. A youngster in the lower grades will be educated that college is in their future and they must begin preparing for it immediately.

Within the first ten years of the enactment of this law, I predict, we will see at least a 25 percent reduction of black folks in the prison population. In 50 years, the percent of black prison inmates will be no more than their proportional percentage in the U.S. population.

There will be a marked increase in employment and in wages earned among the black population and a huge decrease in folks depending on the nation's welfare and social safety net systems (i.e. unemployment compensation, food stamps).

An increase in wages and decrease in unemployment will increase demand of products and services that will stimulate the economy, especially in the black neighborhoods.

All will prosper.

I believe the folks who gave us Jazz, Ragtime, Rap music and the Blues, will give us products and services not yet invented and of unimaginable value to society.

Someone once asked me if I was campaigning to end racism, and I have answered, "No, I am just trying to make racism irrelevant." It is not for black folks that I pray, but for our nation.

In one hundred years, God willing, we shall have lifted the burden of America's original sin off our shoulders and our nation will be absolved. In one hundred years we can say, as truth, in the words of the old Negro spiritual—

> *"Free at last, Free at Last, Thank God Almighty, Free at last."*

Appendix

The Constitution of the United States

Amendment XIII

Abolition of Slavery

Ratified December 6, 1865

Section 1. Neither slavery nor involuntary servitude, except as a punishment for crime whereof the party shall have been duly convicted, shall exist within the United States, or any place subject to their jurisdiction.

Section 2. Congress shall have power to enforce this article by appropriate legislation.

Amendment XIV

Civil Rights

Ratified July 9, 1868

Section 1. All persons born or naturalized in the United States, and subject to the jurisdiction thereof, are citizens of the United States and of the State wherein they reside. No State shall make or enforce any law which shall abridge the privileges or immunities of citizens of the United States; nor shall any State deprive any person of life, liberty, or property, without due process of law; nor deny to any person within its jurisdiction the equal protection of the laws.

Section 2. Representatives shall be apportioned among the several States according to their respective numbers, counting the whole number of persons in each State, excluding Indians not taxed. But when the right to vote any election for the choice of electors for President and Vice-President of the United States, Representatives in Congress, the Executive and Judicial officers in a State, or the members of the

Legislature thereof, is denied to any of the male inhabitants of such State, being twenty-one years of age, and citizens of the United States, or in any way abridged, except for participation in rebellion, or other crime, the basis of representation therein shall be reduced in the proportion which the number of such male citizens shall bear to the whole number of male citizens twenty-one years of age in such State.

Section 3. No person shall be a Senator or Representative in Congress, or elector of President and Vice-President, or hold any office, civil or military, under the United States, or under any State, who, having previously taken an oath, as a member of Congress, or as an officer of the United States, or as a membr of any State legislature, or as an executive or judicial officer of any State, to support the Constitution of the United States, shall have engaged in insurrection or rebellion against the same, or given aid or comfort to the enemies thereof. But Congress may by a vote of two-thirds of each House, remove such disability.

Section 4. The validity of the public debt of the United States, authorized by law, including debts incurred for payment of pensions and bounties for services in suppressing insurrection or rebellion, shall not be questioned. But neither the United States nor any State shall assume or pay any debt or obligation incurred in aid of insurrection or rebellion against the United States, or any claim for the loss or emancipation of any slave; but all such debts, obligations and claims shall be held illegal and void.

Section 5. The Congress shall have the power to enforce, by appropriate legislation, the provisions of this article.

Amendment XV.

Black Suffrage

Ratified February 3, 1870

Section 1. The right of citizens of the United States to vote shall not be denied or abridged by the United States or by any State on account of race, color, or previous condition of servitude.

Section 2. The Congress shall the power to enforce this article by appropriate legislation.

Amendment XXIV.

Poll Taxes

Ratified January 23, 1964

Section 1. The right of citizens of the United States to vote in any primary or other election for President or Vice President, for electors for President or Vice President, or for Senator or Representative in Congress, shall not be denied or abridged by the United States or any State by reason of failure to pay poll tax or any other tax.

Section 2. The Congress shall the power to enforce this article by appropriate legislation.

BIBLIOGRAPHY

Mayer, Jeremy. *Running on Race, Racial Politics in Presidential Campaigns, 1960-2000.* Random House, New York, New York. 2002.

Stiles, T.J. Jesse James, *Last Rebel of the Civil War.* Vintage Books, New York, New York, 2003.

Egan, Timothy. *THE WORST HARD TIME, The Untold Story of Those Who Survived the Great American Dust Bowl.* Houghton Mifflin Company, Boston-New York. 2006

Applegate, Debby. *The Most Famous Man in America, the Biography of HENRY WARD BEECHER.* Three Leaves Press, Doubleday. New York, New York. 2006

Levy, Andrew. *The FIRST EMANCIPATOR, The forgotten story of ROBERT CARTER, the Founding Father Who Freed His Slaves.* Random House, New York, New York. 2005

Oakes, James. *The Radical and the Republican. Frederick Douglas, Abraham Lincoln, and the Triumph of Antislavery Politics.* W.W. Norton & Company, New York-London. 2007

Burton, Orville Vernon. *THE AGE OF LINCOLN.* Hill and Wang, a division of Farrar, Straus, and Giroux. New York. 2007

Simon, James F. *Lincoln and Chief Justice Taney. Slavery, Secession, and the President's War Powers.* Simon & Schuster Paperbacks. New York, London, Toronto, Sydney. 2006

Leman, Nicholas. *REDEMPTION, The Last Battle of the Civil War.* Farrar, Strauss and Giroux. New York. 2006

Dyson, Michael Eric. *DEBATING RACE with Michael Eric Dyson.* Basic Civitas Books, New York, NY. 2007

Rogonsin, Donn. *INVISIBLE MEN, Life in Baseball's Negro Leagues.* Atheneum. New York, 1983.

Tygiel, Jules. *BASEBALL'S GREAT EXPERIMENT, Jackie Robinson and his Legacy.* Oxford University Press. New York. 1983

Richards, Leonard L. *The California Gold Rush and the Coming of the Civil War.* Alfred A. Knoff. New York. 2007

Randall, Willard Sterne & Nahra, Nancy. *FORGOTTEN AMERICANS. 15 Footnote Figures Who Changed American History.* Barnes & Noble. New York, NY. 1998

Beatty, Jack. *AGE of BETRAYAL, The Triumph of Money in America, 1865-1900.* Alfred A. Knoff. New York, NY. 2007

Blumrosen, Alfred W. & Blumrosen, Ruth G. *SLAVE NATION, How Slavery United the Colonies & Sparked the American Revolution.* Sourcebooks Inc. Naperville, Illinois. 2005.

Broyard, Bliss. *ONE DROP, My Father's Hidden Life—A Story of Race and Family Secrets.* Little, Brown and Company. New York, Boston, London. 2007.

Loewen, James W. *LIES, My Teacher Told Me, Everything your American History Textbook Got Wrong.* A Touchstone Book, Simon & Schuster. New York, London, Toronto, Sydney. 1995

Walter Isaacson. *Benjamin Franklin, An American Life.* Simon & Schuster Paperbacks, New York, NY. Page 153

Coontz, Stephanie. *THE WAY WE NEVER WERE, American Families and the Nostalgia Trap.* Basic Books, Perseus Books Group. New York, NY. 2000.

Katznelson, Ira. *WHEN AFFIRMATIVE ACTION WAS WHITE, An Untold History of Racial Inequality in Twentieth-Century America.* W.W. Norton & Company. New York, 2005.

Blackmon, Douglas A. *SLAVERY BY ANOTHER NAME, The Re-Enslavement of Black Americans from the Civil War to World War II.* Doubleday. New York, 2008.

Tatum PHD, Beverly Daniel. *CAN WE TALK ABOUT RACE? And Other Conversations in an Era of School Resegregation.* A Simmons College, Beacon Press Race, Education and Democracy Series Book, Beacon Press. Boston. 2007.

Kaminski, John P. *"THE QUOTABLE JEFFERSON."* Princeton University Press. 2006.

Newton, Jim. *JUSTICE FOR ALL, EARL WARREN and the NATION HE MADE.* Riverhead Books, New York. 2006

Brinkley, Douglas. *THE GREAT DELUGE, Hurricane Katrina, New Orleans and the Mississippi Gulf Coast.* Harper Perennial, New York. 2006.

Roberts, Sam. *WHO WE ARE, A Portrait of America based on the latest U.S. Census.* Times Books, Random House. New York. 1994.

McDonald, Laughlin. *RACIAL EQUALITY.* National Textbook Company, Skokie, Illinois in conjunction with the AMERICAN CIVIL LIBERTIES UNION, New York, NY. 1977.

Shipler, David K. *A COUNTRY OF STRANGERS, Blacks and Whites in America.* Alfred K. Knoff, New York, NY 1997

Ayers, Edward L. *THE PROMISE OF THE NEW SOUTH, Life After Reconstruction.* OXFORD University Press, New York, NY. 1992. Republished 2007.

Hague, William. *WILLIAM WILBERFORCE, The Life of the Great Anti-Slave Trade Campaigner.* Harcourt, Inc. New York, NY. 2007.

Patton, George S. *THE 761ST "BLACK PANTHER" TANK BATTALION IN WORLD WAR II."* Jefferson, NC. McFarland & Company, 1999

Patton, George S. *WAR AS I KNEW IT.* Boston: Houghton Mifflin, 1947.

D'Este, Carlo. *"PATTON, A GENIUS FOR WAR."* HarperCollins Publishers, 1995 NY, NY

Abbott, William F. *THE NAMES ON THE WALL, A CLOSER LOOK.*

Clarke, John Henrik. *PAUL ROBESON, The Artist as Activist and Social Thinker.* Essay.

Gibson, Robert A. *THE NEGRO HOLOCAUST, Lynching and Race Riots in the United States, 1880-1950.*

Kennedy, Stetson. *Jim Crow Guide: THE WAY IT WAS.* Boca Raton, FL. University Press, 1959-1990.

KERNER COMMISSION REPORT, Forty Years After. Eisenhower Foundation Updates, Interview by Bill Moyers of Fred Harris, Former U.S. Senator, Oklahoma and member of Kerner Commission.

Irons, Peter. *A PEOPLE'S HISTORY OF THE SUPREME COURT.* Penguin Books, 375 Hudson Street, N.Y, NY 10014

Lacayo, Richard. *Blood at the Root*. TIME Magazine, April 2, 2002

Gehman, Mary. Louisiana Cultural Vistas Magazine, Winter 2001-2002.

Clotfelter, Charles. *AFTER BROWN, The Rise and Retreat of School Desegregation*. Princeton University Press, 2004

Diuguid, Lewis. Riverside Press Enterprise, January 21, 2008

www.redstone.mil/history www.onlinehelp.com/library/fairhousinghistory]